LOVE LETTER

Guns N' Roses

A Novel
by

Michael Coachella

Copyright © 2015 Michael Coachella
All rights reserved.

ISBN: 0692436618
ISBN 13: 9780692436615
Library of Congress Control Number: 2015915501
MICHAEL COACHELLA, TX

CONTENTS

Chapter 1	Status Quo	1
Chapter 2	Invasion	16
Chapter 3	Classified	25
Chapter 4	Stratagem	31
Chapter 5	Grandiose	36
Chapter 6	Indulgence	46
Chapter 7	Disillusion	67
Chapter 8	Therapeutic Justice	81
Chapter 9	Quixotic Ambition	93
Chapter 10	Kiss Of Death	106
Chapter 11	Abysmal	116
Chapter 12	Penitence	140
Chapter 13	Refresher	150
Chapter 14	Hyperreality	156
Chapter 15	The Crucible	175
Chapter 16	Sabbatical Conquest	185
Chapter 17	Unspeakable	206
Chapter 18	Sacrament	214
Chapter 19	Epiphanous	218
Chapter 20	Catharsis	223
Chapter 21	Coda Monologue	229
Chapter 22	Hedonistic Destiny	231

CHAPTER 1
STATUS QUO

Somewhere in the heart of Texas, I was the everyday, quintessential interpretation of a Type-B personality, and life was just fine. I had just exited the U.S. Army by way of a distinguished honorable discharge with full fiscal retirement benefits. Equally accompanying my vocational achievement was my esteemed life mate, Catharine, whom as a child had acquired the sobriquet of Cat, a multiracial witty southern belle with Asiatic features. Her beauteous appearance was a divergence from her courageous temperament to fight devotedly for the inequity of her virtuousness. During peacetime, she's able to skillfully compartmentalize her combatant alter ego discreetly underneath the cloak of a refined lady with distinguished principles. But whenever she felt the impression that her feminist quality has been infringed upon, she figuratively grabs a sword and swings the forged steel like a shield maiden until she has been vindicated. Nevertheless, she graduated magna cum laude at the local university with a bachelor degree in nursing. She chose her career because she possessed an innate supportive quality to provide care with exhaustive compassion for ailing patients.

Upon my exodus from the Armed Forces, she accepted an offer to work at the premier hospital in the city for a respectable wage as a registered charge nurse in their prestigious department. We celebrated the end of my career and a developing milestone in Cat's profession by moving our family into a comfortable bourgeois community that came equipped with a large, priceless, nineteenth-century Victorian mirror in the living quarters, courtesy of the previous owners who left it behind. Also, to complement my self-esteem, I enthusiastically bought an exorbitant, gasoline-guzzling H2 Hummer to match the erectile organ that anchored my underwear.

Together, Cat and I produced three beautiful, rambunctious children. Aajani, who has an effervescent personality and demands to be treated like a preteen despite a tendency to behave like a sassy infant, is our ten-year-old diva. Then there is our precocious Aaniyah, who is only five years old, but often gets bored with *Dora the Explorer* and strangely prefers to ask collegiate questions. Finally, there's our rough-and-rugged three-year-old named Aalaih, though we usually call her Bamm-Bamm because she likes to beat on things.

Before we settled in, Jackie, a very close friend of mine whom I treasured like a brother, lived only a few houses down on the same street, came over to welcome our family to the neighborhood with a bottle of champagne for Cat and a case of beer for us. A six-foot-five analytical extremist, Jackie instinctively harnessed the technical intellect to understand the schematics of anything that has an operating system. Unfortunately, he lacked the virtue of patience with unanticipated troubleshooting complications, and he was quick to anger when not able to control a viable situation.

Another close surrogate brother of mine named Ronnie tailgated along with Jackie. Ronnie was the president of the local Archangels motorcycle club, and he had the eeriest, lifelike tattoo of an eyeball etched on the outside of both eyelids. Personally, I think it makes him look like a four-eyed freak of nature, since the cosmetic make his eyes look like they're open even when they're closed. But the irony of his physiognomy is he's educated and holds a master's degree in sociology, which validates his pragmatic evaluation of people's characters and also their subterranean agendas.

Counterintuitive to our customary meet-and-greet pledge, we always break the ice with barrages of frolicsome but punishing raw deals of shade-throwing jokes to affirm our esprit de corps. After the battle of witticism on this day, we stood around and discussed my arsenal of weapons inside my newly constructed, territorial man cave I called the Hall of Valhalla, which I personally renovated from a garage to a mecca of NASCAR collector items. My sanctuary was constructed using muscle, blood, sweat, and gears with a lot of testosterone, and the ultra-masculine ornaments were carefully selected with the objective of honoring the most virile of men in mind. Conan the Barbarian himself would consider my dominion a paradise in the heavens for great warriors, complete with an ambiguous sign that complements the milieu, stating, "What is best in life."

I showed the fellas my new twelve-gauge Mossberg pistol-grip pump action shotgun that was recently purchased.

"Is that a new addition to your cache of weapons?" Jackie asked.

Holding it in the upright position, I cocked it so they could witness the characteristic sound from an intimidating weapon of its class, and I said, "This baby sure is!"

"Bro," said Jackie, "you have enough guns and bullets to start a militia and recreate the Battle of the Alamo. Are you sure Davy Crockett wasn't your mother's baby daddy, because you're showing a resemblance right now."

Ronnie burst out laughing like a fool.

"Do you want to know why Ronnie is laughing?" I asked Jackie.

"Why?" Jackie asked.

"Because you look like *Slenderman II*," I told him.

"What?" Jackie asked again.

"That's right, you look like the *Slenderman's* offspring, you terrorizing cyber predator. You and your father should be ashamed of yourselves for stalking the internet and traumatizing teenagers."

Ronnie continued laughing like the Joker, and said, "Damn, you right, all he needs now is his papa's black suit and tie." We erupted in laughter, including Jackie. Ronnie digressed from our lampooning and said, "Man, I love the new vehicle you just bought—that machine is a monster. It fits you."

I couldn't have agreed more and said, "Don't we look alike . . . he's my identical twin. We were separated at birth, but now we're united again. When I take him places, he intimidates the other vehicles, and it gives me an exhilarating rush. I was thinking about buying him a machine gun as a Christmas present so I can mount it on top of the hood and drive around the city with war paint on my face like a commando with PTSD."

Ronnie replied, "Didn't I just see you on *Cops*, driving around naked with an overweight blow-up doll dressed like a hooker in the passenger seat that goes by the name Fuck Me Crazy?"

"Stop dry snitching," I said, "That's so insensitive; the elasticity gives her a low metabolism that she's not proud of. You should be ashamed of yourself for saying that—she's a very lovely girl."

Then on a whim, without provocation, Ronnie awakened the sleeping monster and said, "Has she told you to put a ring on it?"

In my best Gary Coleman voice, I replied, "What you talkin' 'bout, Willis?"

"Don't act like Beyoncé hasn't provided your lady the blueprint of how to wake up with a flawless diamond on her ring finger," he said.

"What you can do with that emasculating idea of yours, Ronnie, is place that propaganda inside Pandora's Box, wrap it with a pretty bow, and ram it up your ass to give yourself a severe case of constipation."

"Mark my words," he said, "Cat is going to make you bow down one of these days and marry her."

I raised my shotgun in the air and propped my left leg on top of an unpacked box like I was the pirate Captain Morgan himself taking a prideful stance on his Second Amendment rights. Using a sound bite from the speech of the late president of the National Rifle Association, Charlton Heston, I retorted with a satirical seriousness, "Not until she removes this piece of steel from my cold, dead hands."

We all laughed at my shameless juvenile shenanigans until we detected Cat's presence at the door. Simultaneously, our laughter subsided when we realized no one knew how long she'd been eavesdropping. Collectively, we mechanically knew that the felony I'd just committed upon her was likely punishable by castration.

Holding a box of light bulbs in her hand, she said, "Don't stop the pandemonium because I showed up . . . what's so funny?"

I lowered my weapon to my side and said, "Nothing, babe, I was only expressing to these fools how much I love this weapon, and we've all been drinking, so you know . . . everything is funny."

"I'm surprised y'all are not out there looking for a rhinoceros to hunt down and kill, so you can cut off its horns to use as a chalice for drinking your prehistoric bonding beverage. Now, that would be comical," she said.

"That's a great idea," I answered sarcastically. "Fellas, get ready, we're going on a safari hunt to slaughter the beast. Babe, plan the expedition for us!"

Jackie held his beer in the air and said, "Touché," and we all gave each other high fives to mock my riposte.

She shook her head with a grin and said, "Boys will be boys . . . if it wasn't for us, you guys would still be dragging your knuckles."

I looked down at the backs of my hands and said, "So that's why I have callouses."

"Please don't quit your day job, because your comedy improv is mediocre," Cat said, rolling her eyes. "But look, I came in here to tell you that this entire pack of new light bulbs blew inside the chandelier you yourself installed, Mr. Handyman."

"Hey, no problem, babe . . . I can have a certified electrician come by tomorrow to check the wiring of that outlet. Would that suffice?"

"Of course. I expect an expensive, handcrafted fixture that was imported all the way from Naples, Italy to work properly."

"Uh, oh," I said, "is that where you think it came from?"

She placed her hands on her hips and said, "Yes, it better have . . . because that's what you told me!"

"Um, how can I say this?" I said, "Well, babe . . . you remember Julio, the guy that used to cut our grass?"

Rolling her eyes again, Cat said, "Umm, hmm."

"I had loaned him fifty dollars once to help him out, and for his debt, he offered me the chandelier that he won from a rooster fight in Tijuana, Mexico."

She stood there looking like a wounded meerkat with the saddest eyes, until I pointed at her and said, "Got you!" She lifted up the box of light bulbs and threw it at me, saying, "Ooh, you get on my damn nerves!" I caught the box with my free hand while the fellas and I cackled like a pack of hyenas at her priceless reaction.

"I'm sorry, babe, but I'll get on it right away," I said while my laughter was tapering.

"You'd better, or you going to find yourself in the doghouse without a bone." I lifted my chin and imitated a wild dog howling under a full moon.

"Oh my goodness, the struggle is real," she said, "Therapy and medication would be useless with someone who clearly rejects help. You should be quarantined so that you don't infect anyone else; your friends are already showing symptoms. But, I'm going to make an exit and leave you three stooges with your regular program."

When Cat left us to our unified proclivities, Jackie said, "I thought you told me that you found it downtown at the flea market?"

I looked over my shoulder to make sure the door was securely shut and said, "I took the gentleman's word when he told me that it was imported from Naples. Just because he was wearing a patch over his eye with six-inch whiskers like a *cholo* doesn't mean that I needed to question his integrity—that's Discrimination 101. So, in theory, I didn't lie. Hell, do you know how much money a person can save at a swap meet by not being too nosey? The name of the game is *don't ask, don't tell.*"

"Man, I know exactly who you talking about," Jackie said. "That *esé* sold me a fucked-up washing machine that cost me more in parts to fix it myself."

Still holding onto my weapon, I flexed and said, "Well, I got this from him too, and I got targets with holes in them the size of Rhode Island that prove this baby is fully operational."

Jackie leaned forward with a scrutinizing gaze and asked to see my shotgun. I handed it to him, and after a moment he said, "This looks exactly like the weapon the last guy who lived here used to blow his brains out."

I heard him clearly, but in disbelief I said, "What?"

Jackie continued, "He had three daughters, like you too."

My persona intensified with austerity, and then I said with an aggressive tone, "Why didn't you tell me someone committed suicide in this house before we moved in, dickhead?"

"It's been vacant for a long time because of it, so I thought you already knew," he said. "Plus I figured your realtor was obligated to tell you about it due to the Freedom of Information Act."

I was flabbergasted. "Oh my goodness, man, are you fuckin' serious?"

"Don't tell me that you believe in all the 'redrum,' superstitious, helter-skelter stuff?" he asked.

"Hell, no," I shot back. "Do I look like a Simple Simon to you? It's not about that anyway. It's about decency, and this so-called Freedom of Information detail, which you neglected to warn me about, tarnishes the whole idea of a peaceful family home."

"Man, I apologize," Jackie said, "but think about it . . . if I never told you about this, life would still be perfect with the unknown and you wouldn't have any worries."

"Well, you screwed that up didn't you, Slingblade? You should've kept that shit to yourself."

"Relax, bro, trust me . . . you don't have anything to worry about," Jackie told me.

"You'd better hope so, since it's too late to do anything about it now. Cat really loves this house, and we're not going anywhere, so don't you dare tell her about what you just told me or even insinuate it. She can never know anything about this. That's a lawful gag order to keep this morbid tragedy quiet."

I grabbed my gun from Jackie and disingenuously said to both of them, "Look, we haven't even broken our home in yet. Y'all instigating plots are already causing strife in my life, so I'm going to need you two blaspheming conspirators to mount your horses and hightail out of my dominion like you've been banished from a great kingdom for heresy."

While they were leaving, Ronnie reminded me of the retro '80s costume party his biker club was hosting at a venue later that evening, saying, "Bro, don't forget to be in character tonight for the Throwback Beat Street Bash."

"Square business, we're going to show up and show out." I told him.

<hr />

Later that night, we made it to the event draped in our fashionable outfits, me dressed in an all-white Adidas sweat suit with black pinstripes down the sides and a pair of all-white Adidas shell-toe shoes, plus two gold-plated dookie rope chains and a pair of clear Gazelle glasses to compliment my face, completing the appearance of a certified hip hop B-Boy. Cat was dressed in a gray *Flashdance* sweat top with pink leg warmers on top of her translucent leggings and pink high heels, plus a multicolored gray/pink headband. When we came through the entrance, our presence turned heads like the demoniacal girl in *The Exorcist*—onlookers gave us expressions of approval and some complimented our coordinated ensemble.

We made our way through the corridor of the entry into the atrium; the entire décor captured the essence of the '80s zeitgeist era flawlessly. The attire, accessories, and vernacular of all the patrons were reminiscent of a jovial, carefree time. The enthusiastic deejay exhilarated the crowd, spinning his gramophonic turntable with the '80s popular funk song "Freak show on the Dance Floor" by The Bar-Kays. I embodied the vivacious urban energetics and lived in the moment while I shimmied my way onto the dance floor with Cat beside me. We extracted renditions of many retro performances out of our throwback repertoire as we could remember. After the dynamic acoustics of the song came to an end, we spoke and jive with some friends we knew.

Thirsty for some nectar of the gods, we headed to the bar, found two empty stools, and copped a seat. I ordered a Hennessey mixed with a Red Bull energy drink, and Cat, with cast-iron certainty, told the barmaid to give her the hardest drink they had on-site.

"Whoa, are you sure about that?" I said.

"Baby, I feel good, and I'm enjoying myself."

I said okay and told the mixologist to give her the business. Cat received her drink, tasted it, and then placed her drink down on the bar and started fanning her tongue.

"What's wrong?" I asked.

"It tastes like piss!" She picked up the glass and said, "Here, taste it."

"How in the hell am I supposed to know what piss tastes like? I'm not tasting that!"

"Well, it does to me, but you may like it . . . come on, taste it."

I grabbed the glass out of her hand and sipped a little bit, spitting it back into the glass. "It does taste like piss—why would you let me taste that?"

"I told you," Cat said.

Turning towards the bartender, I pointed at the glass and told her, "I'm not sure what you put in this drink, but it shouldn't be consumed by humans."

"So I'm guessing you didn't like the Urinalysis Bombshell?" she retorted.

"Who in the hell drinks this on purpose?"

"This is a popular drink among our bikers, and it's not really urine," she informed me. "It's a concoction of several strong liquors, which gives off that tinge of a flavor when combined correctly."

"There's nothing 'correct' about sipping something that tastes like a bedridden patient's urostomy bag from a dialysis clinic—this shouldn't be in nobody's mouth. Give her the next strongest drink that doesn't taste like body fluids, please."

She mixed a new drink and gave it to me; I tasted it first and said, "Wow, Cat, this one tastes like gasoline with a shot of tobacco."

Cat grabbed the glass and said, "I don't care, we're not going to go through this all night with these drinks. Right now, I just need something quick that'll loosen me up. What's the worst thing that could happen? If anything, it'll provide a double purpose to serve us some good: getting me high enough tonight to party like a rock star, and if you run out of gas on our way home, you don't even have to bother finding a 7-11 for fuel. I'll have your supreme unleaded right here inside my bladder, so holla at your girl."

Laughing, I said, "Imagine that . . . my very own sexy service station. Now I'm looking forward to being stranded. Rock on with your bad self."

We were talking and enjoying ourselves for roughly ten to fifteen minutes until some young lady came up and told Cat she was in her seat. Cat told her that we'd been there for ten minutes and she didn't know the seat was already taken. The Madonna lookalike said, "Even if you didn't know, that doesn't excuse a skeezer from asking somebody."

I saw Cat's facial reaction to her response and knew I needed to get involved to relax the situation. "Hey, chill!" I said to Madonna.

She looked at me and said, "I wasn't speaking to you, *dickface*, so go kill yourself!"

Annoyed at the insult, I closed my eyes for a moment to recalibrate and put myself in a better place. Silently I said, *sticks and stones may break my bones, but names will never hurt me.* When I opened my eyes with an emoji smile, she gave me a demeaning jab and said, "I'm sorry, Mr. Cockface, but did you just experience a narcoleptic episode?"

At the moment, I was thinking, *this chick is some kind of crazy— she's probably enrolled in adult day care somewhere because her elevator don't seem to go all the way up.* I kept my composure like I was dealing with an unpredictable outpatient who would have no problem eating her young.

"Okay," I said, you're the Material Girl, right?"

She responded with an irritated sigh. "Hell, no, Madonna is a *bum*. Cyndi Lauper was the baddest bitch!" I apologized for the mix up, advocated to her that we didn't want any trouble, and offered to buy her a drink. She insulted my gesture with an exaggerated hand swipe and said, "You aren't anybody, and you sure don't have enough money to buy me a drink. Get your homely ass out of my face, thinking you cute!"

I thought, *did she just called me ugly in front of everyone . . . hell no, she just fucked up—get her!* I stood up abruptly and said, "Listen, crackhead, for one, your true colors are shining through with too much Vaseline on your hammer head . . . you glistening, but you're supposed to bling with jewels and not with petroleum. Two, that funny-looking wig you rocking make you look like Bozo the fuckin' Clown with bird flu—all you need now is the nose and a magic show, and then that shit still wouldn't be attractive because that motherfucker was never cool. Three, while you were in the bathroom rehearsing "Time After Time" with your Sponge Bob square ass–looking shape, your seat meter ran up, and who in the hell gave you those funky-looking pants anyway, Hulk Hogan? Ding! Ding! Ding! Ding! This next one is extra, so I'm going to need you to pay close attention because it's so disrespectful. Someone give me a drum roll, please."

Some courteous patron sitting on a barstool began tapping on the bar's tabletop to simulate my request.

Then I said, "Now, only a *skeezer* would come out of the ladies' room and walk past a club full of people without knowing that she has doodoo-stained toilet paper trapped on the bottom of her shoe."

People at the bar looked down and noticed the tainted anus tissue and laughed, and I could tell she felt the discomfort of embarrassment that came with contempt when she said, "You're just a zero and a broke, fake-ass L. L. Cool J wannabe. It would have been more convincing if you came dressed up like a food stamp, trick!"

I pulled out a wad of money from my pants pocket that I brought as flash for my B-Boy character and said, "You mad, huh . . . but it's okay, because today is your lucky day. I can tell that you're constipated, and that clearly explains your hostility. You do have my condolences, so how about I pay any clinic of your choice to get that colon cleansed to take all that anger away?" I started peeling off hundred dollar bills, throwing them in the air and saying, "You tell me when to stop, all right . . . first visit, second visit, third visit."

Before I could continue counting my charitable denominations to provide a service for the needy, she ungratefully put a hand on her hip and fanned her mouth, imitating a fake yawn, and said, "I'm bored."

The whiff that I got from the kinetic thrust of her breath was tragic. "That can't be bubble gum—is that roadkill in your mouth smelling like that?" I said.

"It's Skittles, asshole!"

"What a *kawinkydink*, so did they shit in your mouth?"

"Fuck you! Taste the rainbow, bitch!" She had loose Skittles in the palm of her hand, and she placed them inside her mouth and started chewing.

"Let me guess," I said, "you found them on the bathroom floor, right? Did you know that fornicating with a known infection in your mouth is a lustful, deadly sin?" She then spits a colorful, chewy gob of toilet bowl candy at me. In full swing, I swatted it with my hand into the air and yelled, "Home run!"

People around us chuckled. She was hot-tempered and got in my face to confront me about my stroke and then said, "You think you're so fucking funny!"

Our argument continued without interference, both of us were so wrapped up in the brutish grudge match that we were oblivious as to which direction the scattered projectile had gone. All of a sudden during the highlight of our ruckus, I realized that a ginormous, shadowy entity was approaching and blocked out my entire left peripheral space like an eclipse. Without moving my body, I rotated my head as far as my neck would allow me to witness the phenomenon within arm's reach. Once my vision dilated to compensate for the contrasting adjustment, I realized that I'd made an error and mistaken a monstrosity of a woman for a natural occurrence.

She parked her robust physique in front of us and applied her emergency brakes to secure her frame. She sported two sizable afro-puffs and dressed like the Lady of Rage from Death Row Records. At that point, she used both of her hands that were the size of cinder blocks to wipe off the debris dotted on her face and then opened up her big doorway of a mouth and spoke with a guttural, aggressive voice saying, "Who in the hell over here throwing wet Skittles?"

The guys at the bar, myself included, pointed at the Cyndi Lauper ersatz. Cyndi rolled her eyes and said, "What are you going to do about it, pork and beans, coming up in here looking like a blaxploitation African booty-scratching heifer!"

Everybody in the vicinity backed up and waited for the Lady of Rage's up-and-coming fury. I looked into the eyes of the Death Row Records artist and then turned to Cat and said, "Babe, she's ferocious—we're about to see the real *West Side Story*."

"Well, okay," Cat said, "let's see how the West was won." That's when the fuming charade rapper went loco and threw up the "W" symbol with her left hand, drew back with a gangster lean and a forty-ounce Old English 800 malt liquor bottle gripped in her right palm, and threw it toward Cyndi's skull. Cyndi surprised me and displayed some incredible reflexes; she oscillated around the missile with a movement like she was Neo from *The Matrix* without any technical aid from Hollywood's special-effect geeks. She went unscathed while the projectile passed, but the heavy bottle smashed the glass mirror behind the bar with a loud bang, shattering it.

Cyndi balled up her knuckles and got into a bobbing fighting stance like Rocky Balboa and said, "It's time for some action!" She then maneuvered into the inside like a trained fighter and astonished everyone by folding up the robust Lady of Rage with combinations of left and right punches to the gut and then following up with an uppercut to the chin. Shamefully defeated, the Lady of Rage helplessly laid on the floor, knocked out cold, looking like the retired Chicago Bears Refrigerator Perry with puffs of hair sparkling with broken pieces of Skittles like Christmas lights. The only thing that was missing as a headdress was the angel topper ornament, which would've looked nice to welcome the season. I was speechless. The exhibition was so ironic, but then again I was also too impressed to have any ill feelings toward her.

By this time, Ronnie heard the commotion and came over to resolve the situation, but Cyndi was too belligerent at this point to be calmed. So Ronnie had his appointed action-figure musclebound bouncers remove her, kicking and screaming.

"Whatever happened to the girl who just wanted to have fun?" Cat quipped.

Everybody nearby laughed while Cat and I put our glasses in the air to toast our delight as we watched her dramatic exit.

After lowering our glasses down, Cat said, "I love you, baby."

"I love you too," I said.

"I love you more plus one." she said in a challenging nature.

"How about we call it even once you multiply the love that I have for you by one million and a hard-on," I countered.

"Oh, my, you're trying to charm me into something I can't refuse, aren't you?"

"Well," I said, "on L. L. Cool J's *Walking with a Panther* album, he said I'm that type of guy."

"I love it when you talk '80s," Cat replied. "Let's go home and play with each other's Rubik's Cube."

"Classic," I said. "Let's go!"

CHAPTER 2
INVASION

We left shortly after that innuendo exchange, and henceforth inside the vehicle on our way home, Cat said, "Baby, I can't lie, that Cyndi girl was a straight-up hot mess . . . coming to a party looking like a World Wrestling Federation hermaphrodite from the *X-Files*."

I laughed and said, "That's funny, she did look like an androgynous shape-shifter, didn't she? But I'm glad you or I didn't have to fight her—she could've hurt me. She fought like Liu Kang from Mortal Kombat and finished her opponent with his signature fatality without even breaking a sweat. If that knockout was videotaped and uploaded to YouTube, I'm positive she would become the next Internet sensation, even more than Kimbo Slice ever was. Dana White of the UFC would herald her to become the feminine paradigm for a pure specimen of new generational ultimate fighters. I'm telling you . . . she was a trained undercover shaolin assassin; did you see that?"

"Umm umm . . . nope, baby, you didn't have anything to worry about, because I had your back," Cat said from the passenger seat.

"How?" I said, giving her a serious look.

She looked back at me and said, "Look at me . . . I maybe small, but I would've bit her like Tyson."

I laughed as she made biting faces in the air using her teeth. We continued discussing satires and laughed collectively about the particulars during our commute until we got closer to our home. That's when Cat impulsively asked me right out of the blue to stop and get her some cigarettes, which was offbeat because she had never smoked.

"Are you serious, Cat? You don't even like cigarettes, so stop playing."

"I'm serious, Michael. I don't need a whole pack, just a couple. Right now, please."

I was baffled about her apparent seriousness and said, "I'm not stopping to get you no cancer sticks because I don't want to smell the nauseating odor even if you are serious . . . are you okay?"

"I feel intoxicated." she said.

"Yeah, I like it when you're tipsy and want to try new things, but let's leave the cigarettes out of it."

"No, I'm not tipsy . . . I'm drunk!"

"Oh, you white-girl wasted," I said. "Let's get into character and do some naked role-playing when we get to the house. You can paint some freckles on your face, wear that blonde novelty wig that you still have from last Halloween, and call yourself Becky Punani. Then, while you're in the kitchen crying about your anorexic disorder, I'll come into the scene as your therapist, named Johnny-Cum-Lately, and—"

"Not right now, Michael," Cat interrupted, "I'm very drunk, and I'm not joking. I swear I've never felt like this before."

"Okay, but this is a really good one—don't you want to hear the rest of my script?" I asked.

"No, because I don't feel too good. Just take care of me."

I stopped jesting and assured her I would take care of her and conveyed that we would be home in less than ten minutes. Then she collapsed into a drooped posture in the passenger seat.

I pulled up in front of our residence and glanced over at Cat sleeping like a hibernating queen bee. I exited the vehicle, walked around to her side, and opened her door, and then she abruptly woke up and asked, "Where are we?"

"We're home," I said.

Then out of nowhere, a fear descended upon her and her head gyrated in every direction while she frantically screamed, "No! No! No!"

I instantly turned around in a defense manner, concerned that a mob of masked raiders was advancing to hijack my vehicle and cause us harm. But I didn't see anyone, only the panoramic view of the darkling sky. I faced her and grabbed her by her shoulders to get her attention and said, "Stop it! What's wrong?"

With a trembling voice, she said, "I don't want to go in there."

I released her and then stood back and asked, "Are you talking about our house?"

She nodded her head. "Yes."

"Why not?"

"Because there is something inside waiting for me."

"Well, we're not staying out here all night . . . so the motherfucker better be gone before I open the door." I told her.

"It's not leaving." she said.

"It?" I said, puzzled.

"Yes." she said.

I shook my head and got closer and touched her cheek. "Baby, I'm going to secure you better than Allstate. This protection is an insurance policy you can definitely count on; you're literally in good hands." I extended my arms underneath her derriere and pulled her close to me. With her arms crossed over my shoulders and her legs tightly wrapped around my midriff, I carried her toward our front door with a non-slip grip.

I inserted the key into the lock while she held her head down, keeping her eyes closed, and then she whispered, "I'm so afraid."

We got inside our home, and I placed her gently on the sofa and snuggled beside her to provide the security that I promised. She fell back asleep within no time while I prepared to watch back-to-back episodes of HBO's *Cathouse*, filmed at Nevada's notorious brothel called the Bunny Ranch.

After watching several titillating minutes of the erotic program in solitude, I was approved for a bona fide erection. I woke Cat up with a stiff nudge and said, "Hey, meet me in the boom-boom room so we can play *hide-and-go-get-it*."

Cat stretched out her arms to yawn and said, "My mongoose is not servicing you."

I prodded her with my joystick again and said, "Come on, I need some kinky CrossFit exercise tonight, so I can be strong tomorrow."

"The last time we played that game," she reminded me, "you bumped my head underneath the bed, so hell no!"

"Well, can you masturbate me and do that little thing that I like?"

"Nope!"

"You're no fun." I said.

Our conversation was silenced with a long pause until she said, "Um-hum, so you want to have some excitement, huh?"

"Hell, yeah!" I said, thrilled.

She giggled and then said, "You promise not to be afraid?"

"I promise." I then received a delayed, indecipherable comprehension of the question that was posed to me, and I said, "Hold up, are we talking about the same thing?"

"Oomph, I doubt it." she said.

"Okay, I'm confused—how about you give me a tutorial to help me understand?"

She unwrapped my arms from around her and stood up with her back to me and said, "There is something I need to tell you first."

Still lying in the same comfortable position on the sofa, I asked, "What?"

Rigid with a solemn temperament, she said, "Get a Catholic priest. I'm going to need an exorcism because, right now, you're in danger."

After that unsettling caveat, I sat upright on the couch to put some etiquette into my posture. In a bogus, nonchalant manner, I asked, "Why do you believe you need an exorcism?"

Still with her back to me, she unsystematically started crying. "Because I'm possessed with a demonic guest." She appeared to be resolute with her self-evaluation, so I kept my eyes glued to her silhouette and took some time to deliberate her request.

Postponing the pursuit of a priest for a moment, I asked, "Who's your tenant?"

She stopped crying, and then with an unfamiliar tone she answered, "Succubus."

"All right," I said, "I don't want to have sex no more because you just killed my libido with the spookiness . . . and why are you talking about sucking on a bus?"

She lept off her feet to turn and face me with a malevolent gaze and began hissing, and then she uttered a growling vocalization I've never heard pitched from her voice and said, "I'm a demoness, you ignorant heathen!"

I could hear my heart beating in my throat while I attempted to swallow my retreating saliva. I held my hand up in submission and said, "Okay, I'm sorry. How did we come into contact with a demoness?"

"This house possesses a precious conduit that has a portal with direct access to hell," she answered.

"So why did you choose Cat?"

"Because she's my vessel for getting close to you."

"Huh? What do you want with me?" I asked.

She pointed at me and said, "I'm going to destroy you and bring you to your knees."

Embarrassingly intimidated, I muscled up my bravado and told her firmly, "Watching that crap on television don't qualify you to be a demon no matter how many times you've seen it, so you need to stop playing!"

She gave me an evil stare with penetrating eyes and said, "I want to show you something."

Nervously, I asked, "What do you need to show me?"

She leaned her torso forward, coming closer to me, and then whispered, "I'm going to levitate for you." Instantaneously, I felt a hypothermic rush as goose bumps surfaced on my skin, and I gulped the shallow amount of oxygen that was diminishing between our neighboring faces. I instinctively leaned away from her, and though I was extremely frightened internally, I did my best to restrain those fears with my exterior disposition.

I was still cowering when she said, "You don't want to miss this."

Then she took a couple of steps back, gesticulated her bestowed omnipotence by extending her arms out to the side like a crucifixion, and then tilted her head back while closing her eyes. I was petrified now as she fixed herself in position to prove to me that I was in the presence of something truly evil. She began reciting an inaudible chant in some form of language I couldn't decipher. I was stoned in fear while I scrutinized every detail of her figure and whispered to myself, "Please don't levitate." Reciting those words over and over again didn't alleviate my trepidation, it exacerbated the realness of the situation, because my heart was jumping over

Olympic size track hurdles, engulfed in flames inside my chest. I felt reluctantly compelled to watch the enigmatic phenomenon because my vision was paralyzed with terror. All of a sudden, she stopped and said, "You're an infidel and don't deserve to witness my supreme power." At that moment, I was honored to be a heretic and very relieved it didn't happen.

Tasting oxygen again after temporarily holding my breath, I shouted, "What the fuck was that all about?"

"You'll find out," she said.

"What the hell am I going to find out?"

She walked toward the guest bedroom and said, "You'll see."

I got up off the couch and followed her into the room and asked her what will I see, but she didn't respond as she crawled into the bed, got underneath the sheets, and stared at me with an ocular threat in addition to an ice-cold smile grimacing across her face.

"Okay," I said, "I'm getting the fuck out of here!"

I entered the garage, got a suitcase, went into the master bedroom that we share, and locked the door behind me. I placed the open suitcase on the bed and began packing necessities for my stay at a local hotel. While standing over my luggage, I heard a humongous bang on the bedroom door behind me. It startled and frightened me so badly that I skedaddled across the room, but the bioelectric system in my brain didn't coordinate fast enough with my lower extremities, immobilizing my feet while my torso was in motion and caused me to tumble to the floor. I immediately jumped up, hustled to the door, unlocked, and opened it. But I didn't see Cat or anyone when I scanned the living room quarters, nor did I see anything out of place. I stood there for a moment and scratched my head, and then I said to myself, *damn, I know I'm not trippin'*. I turned around to go back into the room to finish packing. That's when I saw that the door was damaged. Livid,

I said, "All right, these childish shenanigans have to stop. I've had enough of this shit!"

I swiftly walked over to the guest bedroom where Cat was, and she was awake, lying on her back in the same spot beneath the sheets looking at me with those same piercing eyes.

Clapping my hands to emphasize my demand, I said, "Okay, this hocus-pocus foolishness stops right now . . . you cracked the fuckin' door!" She broke her stare, and her eyes began to roll as I heard a curdling, sinister laugh coming from her. I lost it and jumped on top of her, pinning her arms underneath the sheets, and began choking her. "I'm your priest now," I told her, "and this is the exorcism you asked for!" She was still trying to laugh, so I proceeded to slap her across the face like they do in the movies when this happened.

Just as a succession of strikes came raining down for compliance, she coherently looked at me and said, "Michael, what are you doing?" I stopped my assault in midair when I realized she was self-aware, rolled off her, and sat on the side of the bed, discombobulated.

"Why were you slapping me?" she demanded.

I looked at her in disbelief and said, "Don't you remember?"

"Remember what?"

"The things you were saying about Succubus, and levitating?"

Bewildered, she said, "Who is Succubus? The last thing I remember is leaving the '80s costume party. I don't recall us making it home."

The following day we discussed what happened in more detail to understand what caused her to black out. I apologized to Cat for striking her while she was incoherent, and expressed how the ordeal was by far the eeriest paranormal event I'd ever witnessed, and how I hoped to never experience it again.

"If you were so terrified, why didn't you get a priest like I asked?"

"Well, I didn't have time to go looking for one because I thought your head was about to start spinning like that chick in *The Exorcist*, so to prevent your neck from turning like a merry-go-round, I acted as an honorary priest that was granted full authority to drive that maleficent entity out."

"How did you get ordained so fast?" she asked.

"The Archangel Saint Michael came down and anointed me on the spot, giving me full dominion to abuse your flesh for one night only." I laughed, but she said it wasn't funny.

We continued deliberating the matter, trying to determine how the anonymous alcoholic beverage was correlated with the unexplained temporal neurotic supernatural possession. Our only fathomable explanation was that our hyper-imaginative fears were taken out of context, which allowed our reality to become ghastly exaggerated. We also decided, for peace of mind and closure about the mysterious and creepy subject, that we would never talk about it again.

CHAPTER 3
CLASSIFIED

One day Jackie stopped by to pick me up to visit the shooting range and enjoy the camaraderie of dispelling gun smoke from our big-boy toys. I love the fact that society has condoned an establishment where men can go and release our barbaric tendencies and parade our masculine alter ego in a safe, controlled environment. I believe most men need a periodic archaic form of release as an antidote, to be able to function appropriately without incident in this contemporary developed society. At least, until each antiquated individual like myself is cultivated and competent enough to be pliable within a sophisticated, idealistic-driven society of nonaggressive intellectuals we're humanizing more to become.

With the ever pursuit of sensation-seeking, the video-gaming industry has capitalized on a formula for delivering virtual stimulation. The effectivity of their commercialization grossed the industry a record-breaking eighteen point five billion dollars in revenue in 2011. Violence is profit. Even now, the most ultraviolent video games are the hottest commodity among children and adults. I saw a study indicating that more adults play video games than kids because the first generation of gamers are still the core generation for marketing, and every year some teenager is being inducted into this vast community of adult gamers. Maybe simulated video games that promote criminality and licentious behavior should be treated like controlled substances. This alternative will allow registrants with deviant interests to safely indulge in their fantasies privately, so their nefarious compelling urges can be met until other conscionable methods could be implemented. I believe a methodical approach to this option, with caution and safeguards, could decrease crime in my relative, paradoxical opinion.

On the ride back home, Jackie said, "I got something to tell you—guess what!"

I looked at him and said, "You're pregnant!"

"Man I swear you're a fuckin' idiot," he said. "How in the hell did you get this far in life?"

"With the extraordinary talent of taking nothing serious."

"Well, that philosophy is contingent upon what I have to say next."

"Try me," I said.

He briefly removed his hands from the steering wheel and popped his knuckles before he continued. "First, let me ask why you get defensive and flippant when we bring up marriage around you."

"Oh my goodness, I'm really starting to get aggravated about y'all bringing up this marriage foolishness . . . come on, man, let it go."

"I'll tell you what," Jackie said. "If you can give me a serious answer for once without making a joke out of it, I'll never ask you about it again."

I thought for a moment and said, "Bet, I'll tell you. I think marriage is superficial, overvalued, and unnecessary. The saying 'a happy wife is a happy life' is bullshit. Who's coming up with this silliness? That type of selfishness is biased against the fellas. Whatever happened to equal opportunity?" Imitating Tony Montana from *Scarface*, I said, "What, you want me to stay there and do nothing? I'm no fuckin' criminal, man. I'm no puta or thief. I'm Tony Montana, a political prisoner from Cuba . . . and I want my fuckin' human rights now. Just like the President Jimmy Carter says, okay?"

"See, that's what I mean," Jackie said. "You can't ever give a complete answer without making a comedy out of it."

I laughed. "Come on now, dick itch, you know that was funny. It was good timing, wasn't it?"

"Look, bro, you need to stop jiving around and take this serious."

"Why?" I asked him.

"I'll tell you . . . but first, let me get my brush and paint a picture for you. I know that you love her, but are you *in love* with her?"

"Yeah." I said.

"Do you believe that she feels the same way about you?"

"Shit, I hope so." I paused briefly and then said, "Hold up, I take that back . . . she does. As a matter of fact, she probably loves me even more."

"Okay, when you truly love someone, and you know wholeheartedly that person you're in love with loves you back just as deeply, the best gift that you can give each other is your faith in marriage. That's assurance in the proverbial right here and right now. That sacred, symbolic gesture is showing each other 'I love you forever with totality,' and you're both oblivious to a future of uncertainty because in your heart of hearts, for right now, you know your love for this other person is irreplaceable and will last for eternity."

"Wow, that picture you just painted looks like a Picasso . . . is that how you feel about Lynda?"

He gave me a very sincere look. "I knew she was the one, so it was destined for us to become the two. When she gave birth to our daughter Jalyn, we became an everlasting trinity. I love them more than anything that you or I could ever imagine."

"So, y'all have a picture-perfect relationship, huh?"

"Maybe not to others. But it's as perfect as perfect gets for us, because we put a hundred percent into giving each other satisfaction. Most of the decisions we make are decided contingently upon taking each other's feelings into a 360-degree consideration, in hopes of providing us an entire sphere of understanding. When we hit any challenges due to any harmless personal motivations or some type of legitimate difference, we have mutually agreed to compromise our disagreements by flipping a coin and letting fate decide."

"Man, you too fly . . . really? Y'all flip a coin, for real?"

"Yeah, it works, and we both honor it too . . . one quarter is all it costs to keep down confusion. But it's not that often that we have to do that, because we share a lot of the same interests and do enjoyable things together. We get along great."

"That's amazing," I said, "I'm sure y'all must be happy."

"Happiness is secondary to the euphoria I feel every moment knowing, without a doubt, that the special union I share with my wife is unbreakable and forever."

"Wow, what y'all have is very special. That's what I want."

Jokingly, he said, "You can't have what I got, because my wife belongs to me exclusively, but you can make your relationship with Cat congruent to what I have."

"That's what I'm talking about, fool!" I quipped.

Jackie then rubbed his hands together and said, "Now that I have your attention on this subject and you're agreeable, I need to let you know why I've been questioning you about marriage lately."

Looking at him with a curious expression. "Why . . . ?"

He told me that Cat and his wife had had a conversation not too long ago, and Cat had told her if I didn't marry her within the next twelve months, she would leave me. I was agitated to hear him say that, so I told him to stay out of my business. He held up his hands and said, "Hey, don't shoot the messenger."

I stared at the side of his errand-boy-looking face and said, "You're not *Paul Revere,* don't give me that crap, man!" I took a break from the exchange to count automobiles that were passing in the opposite lane to detour from the newsflash that just broadsided me like a demolition-wrecking ball. After counting ten vehicles, I said, "I can't believe that she would betray me like that, and do something so drastic just because we're not married yet."

"Well, you have nine more months left."

"Nine months for what?"

"Do you need subtitles? To be married, fool!"

"I'm not as dumb as I look. I thought you said twelve months?"

"That was three months ago," he said.

"You breaking all the rules, going against the grain . . . give me those wings back, because you ain't fly at all. What type of guy would keep that from his brother for three months? You're coldblooded."

He extended his right hand and told me, "A brother that will be there and stand with you as your best man." Our hands united as we gave each other a silent agreement. Then I informed him there is a secret about me that Cat was unaware of, and that the undisclosed material needed to be resolved before there were any chances of us getting married.

"Man, I know everything there is to know about you, so what are you talking about?"

"Bro," I said, "even you don't know anything about this."

"Really? So what the fuck is it?"

"Not now. This shit is too heavy to hold, and too hot to touch."

He looked at me like I was a stranger. "I've known you for almost ten years. What are you, an FBI most-wanted fugitive? Don't tell me you're a black fascist Nazi communist?"

"I could only wish that was my problem, because I would rather face the government with your cockamamie story than face Cat with mine. But I got us involved in some twisted talk-show shit."

"I knew it—you're into that freaky-deaky bestiality stuff, aren't you? Which furry costume you like playing dress-up in?"

I looked at him and said, "Barney, the purple dinosaur. We just had our annual convention at the Marriott Hotel last month. But let's keep all of this between us until I can break it to Cat."

"Man, I was only joking—are you fuckin' serious?"

"Hell, nawl," I said. "Get the fuck out of here accusing me of *your* embarrassing guilty pleasures. What do you think I am, a goddamn degenerate?"

"No, a pervert. I was about to drop your ass off at the police station."

"See, you need to stop profiling. I only look like this." I then ended our sarcasm by expressing to him that it wasn't the appropriate time to disclose classified information about my predicament. Furthermore, I informed him that everything would be copacetic, and I'd brief him about what was going on later with the cessation of cleaning out my closet.

CHAPTER 4
STRATAGEM

To meet my deadline, I needed to figure out an expeditious way to inject an effective dose of anesthesia to lessen Cat's sensitivity before delivering the pain. The goal of my exploit was to symbolically bulldoze the earth-shattering debris from our terrain with some inventive heavy machinery and then restructure a newly secure infrastructure with a balanced foundation. After doing a series of mental gymnastics through my deductive reasoning, I contrived an elaborate, antagonistic plot in a sequence of three stages that would become the blueprint to this labyrinth strategy. The covert operation that I named *Stratagem* was an ingenious plan that incorporated resentment, retaliation, and the finale, which would entail the revelation. Since I was under a strict time restraint, I didn't have the convenience of commissioning an outside general for the task of overseeing the operation. So I recruited from within for a courageous soldier, and I then empowered my alter ego to step up and volunteer his civil service. He accepted the challenge with gratitude and honor, along with being granted the noble titles of commander-in-chief, down to the infantry scout to serve and protect the union. I was already in possession of all the logistical material needed to aid me with my advantageous assignment to streamline this urgent process. The only foreseeable concern was that collateral damages were to be anticipated, but I rationalized the benefit would atone for the house of cards collapsing to the ground.

I initiated the first stage of my mission while Cat was sound asleep next to me one night. I low-crawled out of bed into the living room to the desktop computer and logged on to my social media page to begin trolling for a flirtatious cyber affair with a lucky candidate as my unsuspecting decoy. I quickly entangled a young lady into my ambush, who was either captivated by the charm of my keystrokes or naiveté about the clichéd pickup lines. We were both caught up in the rapture of our many lustful conversations and carried on the illicit courtship for many days.

Early one Saturday morning, about a week into my scandalous philandering cyber chat, I put on my military-grade camouflage cap and decided it was time for phase one to come into fruition. I woke the kids up and got them excited to hurry up and get dressed by telling them that I was taking them to the local Bounce and Jump facility for children, which was the code name for the Staging Area. Before we left, I logged onto my social media page and intentionally left it unsecure while Cat was still in bed, hoping that she would check my message journal to give her an alarming rise and shine. My calculated expectation was to set an ambiance in the room for a one-sided confrontation upon my return, which would provide me the opportunity to show my false contrition.

At the assembly point, the kids were about an hour into their playtime while I watched them from the lobby section that was outfitted with chairs and sofas for visiting parents. I found myself listening to two women's dramatic conversation about their urchins. A Herculean-size lady who resembled Madea complained to her friend about her child's recent behavior and declared that she was going to punish her son severely if she caught him doing what he had done or even heard that he was doing it. I was so intriguingly involved in the conversation to find out what her son's offense was that it took me a moment to realize that Cat's Cadillac Escalade was whipping into the parking lot like a Japanese kamikaze fighter pilot swooping down on Pearl Harbor for a rematch.

She exited the automobile clutching papers, still wearing pajamas and fuzzy slippers, with a disheveled head of hair making her look like she'd stuck her finger inside a light socket with a million and one volts. I panicked and sprung to my feet, because my mission was compromised, but I screamed in distress to myself, *no, not here . . . abort, abort, abort!* Right before she entered the building, I deviated from my battle plan and sprinted down the center lane of the play area. Looking for concealment, I dodged behind a huge Godzilla bouncy in the rear of the place. I looked around and saw a kid pointing at me, screaming "Stranger danger! Amber alert!"

"Shut your mouth. I'm not a pervert, you little fucker!" She antagonistically stuck her tongue out, and I attempted to get away from the brat and move to a more concealed cover; however, my left hamstring muscle cramped up with an excruciating charley horse, preventing me form moving anywhere. I went down to the floor, grabbing the leg that immobilized me with a spasm, and temporarily thought about surrendering. But I just couldn't tap out like a defeatist, and I wished I could've dug a man-size tunnel like a die-hard Vietcong guerrilla from underneath the spot I was squatting all the way home, but then again, I didn't have time to ask the staff for a shovel. So, I had to think fast and improvise, due to my oversight of a contingency plan.

I then noticed another random kid in my vicinity with his hands down his pants playing with himself. I said, "Hey kid, come here." The little boy looked surprised and corrected himself before he came over, and I asked him, "Where is your mother?" He pointed out his mom by the entrance. I grabbed him by his arm and said, "Yep, that's her. I saw what you did, and I'm taking you to her right now, because you're in big trouble." I picked him up and he immediately began to beg me not to tell her and promised to never do it again for the rest of his life. I said, "Well, it's too late for that." I was able to make it all the way to the seating area close to the front door with the camouflage assistance of the little masturbator. I delivered the kid to his mother as a disposable accessory and said, "He did exactly what you told him not to do." I then exited the building undetected.

 I pulled up to our home and hastily darted inside to prepare for the calculated fiasco. While I waited on Cat's incoming nuclear warhead, I briefly thought about my shameless intrusion between the kid who got caught in the crossfire and his mother. But, the timing with his transgression against himself coincidentally became an asset, which certainly provided me the assistance to escape my compromising position. The kid probably deserved a Purple Heart medal for his service, but the young, aspirant Jack the Ripper should've been thrown into the brig for his publicized sexual assault on his tallywacker.

 Standing in the main quarters of the house, I waited, anticipating Cat's arrival to be like a battering ram penetrating through an obstacle people called a front door. I heard a commotion on the other side of the barricade as I stood in front of the television pretending to channel surf for something to watch as a diversion. Then I thought, *let's get ready to rumble,* as she breached the confines of the structure with a metallic device called a key and entered the premises. Before I could even see her, it was obvious she was enraged because I could hear the contemptuous stomps in her marching rhythm. I was prepared with my rules of engagement when she appeared from around the foyer. But I'm sure my unflappable demeanor only accelerated her verbal assault as she threw the sheets of contraband in my face that held detailing conversations between me and the cooperative. She stood in front of me, placed her hands on her hips like a crass mad black woman from a Tyler Perry stage play, and discharged a battering condemnation.

"I can't believe you did this to me. You promised that you would never cheat on me, you lying bastard!"

I nodded and simply said, "Roger."

"You messed up."

Again I nodded. "Roger."

"I've been loyal to you the entire time."

When I nodded a third time with a "Roger," she said, "Why in the hell are you calling me Roger? Isn't that a military term?"

"Yes," I told her. "I was just trying to show you some respect."

"Don't patronize me with that ridiculous jargon!"

"Okay."

"Tell me, why would you take me for granted?"

"I'm sorry," I said. "I made a mistake."

She pointed at me, saying, "And that mistake is going to stalk you like the bubonic plague. Good luck, asshole. I have our children whom you recklessly abandoned like the selfish prick that you are." As she was leaving she said, "FYI, you are not in the military any longer, and I'm not your trooper, so take that dumb-ass camouflage hat off because it doesn't even match!" Then she slammed the door in a dramatic exit.

CHAPTER 5
GRANDIOSE

Before entering stage two of my trilateral modus operandi, there was a necessitating criterion to fulfill in order to calm the storm. Since nothing says I'm sorry like money, I bought her an expensive pair of red-bottom, five-inch-heel Christian Louboutin stilettos, along with an exclusive Prada purse as reparations for my atonement in order to proceed to the next phrase. Gifts of this nature must possess a mystical whip appeal, because men have utilized this very tactic for thousands of years. I can imagine a Neanderthal male committing a prehistoric form of infidelity and redeeming himself by delivering a twelve-foot woolly mammoth tusk to his bristly queen as a peace offering. And the dirty-faced cavewoman acting nonchalant about the gift until her pack of girlfriends says, "Girl, that caveman is crazy about you . . . you'd better keep him."

I was exonerated for my criminous behavior with the forfeiture of my Facebook passcode as a precondition that allowed Cat to perform periodic checks and balances, verifying that I was no longer involved in transgressive activities. After reaching this juncture, the state of affairs required me to demilitarize my militant alter ego's disposition, because the actions of the second stage only obligated me to lease out tedious patience with a watchful eye for retaliation. I implemented a low-level homeland security tactic, effectively blending into my surrounding environment as a non-combatant civilian with the objective of observing and collecting pertinent intelligence for the command center.

Two weeks after the inception of *Operation Stratagem*, I checked Cat's Facebook page and detected that she had made a mutinous enemy contact with an undesirable target; as a result, I annotated the intelligence into my mental check-log for a collective debriefing at a later date. Despite the fact that I remained in character with a copacetic attitude toward the nature of the offense, I was extremely jealous. But I fully understood that it was important for me to keep up the fictitious facade of cluelessness and not expose my detestation of this forbidden friendship. So unfortunately, it was crucial that I allow the nature of the birds and the bees to escalate into a lascivious tryst.

To prevent myself from getting emotionally capricious and undermine the grand design before it could manifest, I gave an executive order to my increasing sensitivity to take an indefinite leave of absence as a safeguard. At that point and time, and with a disengaged heart, I projected that the time expectancy should be ephemeral before the third stage came into fruition, which would provoke my subterranean secrecy to be publicized.

I continued monitoring my subject and the target fraternization for another month, engaging into platonic communication until it was abruptly disconnected. Without any other communication monitoring that I could observe from electronic devices, I delegated the ongoing assignment to my instincts to continue the undercover operation for future developments.

A couple of months later, with no sign of subversive activity, I assumed that Cat had abandoned her reprisal. All the ingenuity and effort that I managed to stage for the finale to crystallize into a masterful work of art appeared to be an unsuccessful battle plan. I was unable to pull off the confrontation with my hidden agenda. So I placed my mission on inactive status until I could reassess the ineffective fragment of my orders and revamp the narrative to something more effective that would evoke Cat to react. With Saint Valentine's Day approaching and a congenial atmosphere surrounding us, I postponed my timetable so that I could make preparations to show Cat a token of my affection.

On the day of love, I made arrangements and reservations for a secluded, romantic play date for the entire day. We began our midday outing with an almost relaxing visit to a Japanese acupuncturist's shop that stuck ultrathin needles inside our carcasses, as an ancient therapeutic technique to harmonize our bodies' natural yin and yang forces. After the physical therapy, we followed up the rest of our afternoon with an eloquent dinner at a notable seafood restaurant and then watched a romantic movie at a historic cinema that showcased classic films. The diurnal course of the evening was eventful, despite Cat's commitment with a trivial annoyance of occasionally texting her older sister. When I questioned the cellular distraction, she explained a needfulness to assist with the preparation of her mother's welcoming home itinerary from a vacation abroad.

Later that evening, we arrived back home to unwind and pleasure each other with an uninterrupted adult game of Sugarland like we were sexual diabetics in heat. I entered the kitchen to finish my leftovers from dinner and informed Cat I'd be in shortly when she entered the master bedroom to shower and prepare for a shameless night of *I'll never tell* activities.

After satisfying my culinary appetite, I made my way to the bedroom. When I opened the door, I was overwhelmed by a sensational ambush. Cat's perfectiveness in embodying the seductive attribute of the goddess Venus was pictorially spellbinding to my sensory. I paused for a moment to appreciate the beauty of the effeminately constructed sanctuary. "Love Faces" by Trey Songz vocalized softly through the speakers. A few white candles flickered and harmonized with the red rose petals placed around the room. Cat had immaculately captured the sexual mood right out of the erotic novel *Fifty Shades of Grey*. It was electrifying, and I was thrilled because I knew that I was in for a vigorous night of Kama Sutra Olympics. My eyes penetrated Cat standing across the room with her right foot placed on top of the footstool to accentuate her figure. She looked like a centerfold vixen, in a sanguine-colored corset with straps connected to a coordinated pair of transparent stockings. Michelangelo must have sculpted the fine fabric on her petite curves as an ageless timepiece for his final encore. She used an ostrich whip and motioned me to come over and occupy the footstool next to her. I was mesmerized, and everything felt cinematic as I drifted into several frames of slow motion escorted by her attractiveness. I obediently made my way to the appointed position as she victimized me with a stimulating striptease that was delightfully enticing. I endorsed her entrapment by submitting physically, and respected my unadulterated thoughts by enjoying every moment of my captivity. After the chorus came close to an end, she executed her flawless performance with a passionate kiss and then whispered to me, "I have something waiting for you in the bathroom." She pulled back, cracked her whip, and then strutted her way onto the bed with the grace and stealth of a wild feline.

I entered the restroom with assurance until I saw that Cat had acquired me a red edible thong resembling an athlete's jock strap so my buttocks could hang out the back like a donkey's ass. The procurement of this article of contraband was blasphemous twenty-five hours a day, eight days a week, and righteously punishable by a good Old Testament stoning.

I opened the door, held it up, and said, "Come on, what is this inappropriateness . . . are you serious?"

She swiped her hand as if she had clawed nails and rolled her tongue like Eartha Kitt in her famous Catwoman role of the *Batman* television series and said, "Purr-fect for one night only, Batman."

I closed the door and deliberated for a moment over the thought of having the fleshy part of my hindquarters unprotected. Grudgingly, I went ahead and made the hard decision to appease her but made a promise to get myself some compensation for the terroristic threat against my machismo.

I refreshed myself with a shower, dressed my loins with the incomplete, deplorable gift, and appropriately doused myself with an aromatic amount of Hugo Boss cologne. Now prepared for a bonanza of obscene pleasures, I exited the restroom into the disappointing milieu of Cat's unresponsiveness to my entrance, because she was now sleeping beneath the sheets. My attitude was unperturbed, as I knew she was understandably fatigued from the marathon of events that enduringly encompassed our adventurous day. When I made my way to motivate her cognizance to an elevated arousal of my presence, I heard her cell phone chirp, indicating a new message. I was curious as to why Cat and her sister were texting that late, so I picked up her phone from the top of the bed rest and casually attempted to crack the numerical security code to allow me access. I received many unsuccessful *try again* alerts before I tried something more personal, as in the last four digits of her social security number. Then, like a sorcerer—I said the magical words, "Abracadabra, alakazam." Voilà! I was granted permission to explore the unknown depth of mystery without prejudice, because the proprietor of the device was sound asleep in the proverbial la-la land of sweet dreams.

I retrieved the text message, and the phrase *I love you too* displayed across the screen. I looked at the receiver box and noticed that the message was generated from the undesirable perpetrator.

Suddenly I dropped the phone like an exploded grenade and rubbed my eyes, because the visualization of those words felt like shrapnel had lodged into my sockets. All of my facilities began ringing the alarm and screamed *Mayday! Mayday! Mayday!* The muscles in my throat restricted my airwaves and cut my lungs off from the oxygen that I needed to sustain consciousness. Lightheadedness compromised my ability to steer myself to safety, and my legs began to wobble because they were too weak to hold the weight of the cargo. Before I crash-landed like a 747, my copilot received the distress signal and took over the flight, saving my valuable fuselage. With a pep talk, I encouraged myself to maintain my equilibrium and then I picked up the phone to validate that my eyes weren't deceiving me. The message was still there in the palm of my hand, appearing enlarged; it might as well have been decorated on a life-size billboard with flashing neon lights to express his feelings. There was a mutiny on deck, and I was oblivious to this treacherous act being remotely possible when I constructed my mental spreadsheet for all involved risk assessments. I scrolled down and observed her prior text expressing her related sentiments that initiated his response. Continuing my espionage of the electronic device, I discovered that she had been communicating with him all day, not collaborating with her sister for her mother's return. Regretfully, I had implanted an insidious plot that was detrimental to my emotional security, which now confirmed a broken heart. There wasn't a military-grade protective vest designed that could protect my emotions, or a medic with extensive training able to mend the rip, nor were there any anesthetics developed that could make the pain go away. With all the strength seemingly depleted out of my once vibrant body, I attempted to get my equanimity recalibrated but failed miserably as my fragility indicated weakness in my attempts to wake her.

After a few unsuccessful attempts to awaken her to confront this monstrous debacle, she finally woke up and noticed my contemptuous demeanor and said, "Babe, I'm sorry I fell asleep on you, but I got so tried waiting. Are you okay?"

I felt like she was antagonizing me by asking that after what I'd just witnessed, and that show of disrespect encouraged my interrogating posture. With the indisputable evidence in my hand to convict her of the heinous crime, I reached out and extended her phone within a legible distance from her face and ask firmly, "What is this?"

She looked at it for a moment with eyes suggesting, at first, that she needed an escape route to the moon, but she decided to give it to me raw and said in a scornful tone, "How does it feel?"

Discombobulated by her answer, I said, "What the hell does that mean?"

She leaped out of bed on the opposite side with the gaze of a vindictive tigress. "An eye for an eye!"

At that point, we got passionately involved in a melodramatic battle of the sexes. There were reciprocated exchanges of verbal assaults, with indictment charges thrown at one another during our linguistic attack. Then suddenly, in the heat of the moment, my professionalism kicked into gear. I was reminded of my initial intention in orchestrating the plan in the first place. Even though it turned out to be a fiasco, I acknowledged the good in the opportunity and sidelined my emotions that caused me to become complacent, and I seized the moment by interrupting our altercation.

"There's something I need to tell you that's gargantuan in comparison to what you've done."

She abruptly stopped and said, sarcastically, "What, you got a baby?"

"I sure do . . . and she's eight years old." I said, with a smirking expression.

Even though she'd suggested it with sardonicism, she wasn't prepared for the truth, and she became overdramatic and screamed out, "I'm going to kill you!"

She ran out of the bedroom into the Hall of Valhalla, headed for the armory that stored all the weapons. I knew I couldn't let her open the safe, so with the temporary quickness of Carl Lewis, I sprinted as hard as I could and arrived there while she was at the keypad, trying to enter the security code. I grabbed her from behind and lifted her up into the air, attempting to remove her as far from the safe as possible. She was kicking and screaming, saying, "Put me down! I'm going to fucking kill you!"

I put her down on the floor in a location that placed me between her and the gun safe, but I still had my arms tightly around her and said that I would let her go if she would relax. She stopped her tirade, and I released my grizzly-bear hug. She turned around to face me and said, "Keep your fucking hands off of me!"

With the threat under control, I held my hands in the air as a hopeful indicator that our scrimmage was over. We were both breathing heavily, watching each other's every move, and then she dashed over to the wall and snatched the spare key fob to her vehicle. I stayed in my position, because I didn't recognize her action as being dangerous. She then pushed the button above the key caddie to open the garage door.

Cat walked out of the garage toward her vehicle and said, "Fuck you. I still have a loaded weapon inside my car."

I was exasperated, and I wanted firepower for myself to combat her threat. I leaped to the safe in a single bound like I was Superman and quickly entered the security code as fast as I could. I reached inside the safe after I opened the door and pulled out my loaded AK-47 assault rifle with an extended magazine. I turned around and ran to the entrance of the open garage and chambered a round with the barrel of the rifle pointing to the floor on my right side just in case she was bluffing. Our eyes locked menacingly onto each other like a pair of nemeses in an old Twentieth Century western standoff. She had backed down and retreated from my opposing show of force, when she suddenly placed her vehicle in reverse, backed out of the driveway into the street, and stopped.

Feeling victorious, I gave her a condescending smirk and said, "Yeah, you know what's up. You better get your scary ass out of here. You weren't going to do shit!" She then rolled down her window and poked out her tender lips, gave me a lovable smile like Bambi from the Walt Disney pictures.

I can't believe after all of that, she's about to ask me if we can be friends, I thought. So I dropped my guard, prepared for us to call a truce and make up. Cat then said, "Come here, sweetheart."

I had started approaching her car when she audaciously double-crossed me and pulled out a Smith & Wesson stainless steel .44 Magnum revolver, pointed it at me, and started shooting like she was a gangland enforcer. I quickly turned, zigzagging my way back into the garage for refuge, and ducked around a corner inside Valhalla. Then I heard her tires screech against the asphalt as she pulled off.

I immediately came from my secure hideout holding my weapon, infuriated, and I sprinted down the street barefooted and clothed only in a thin licorice thong, along with a supreme grade of booty meat slapping in the wind like a pair of flapjacks. When I got within the kill zone, I quickly slowed to a complete stop in the middle of the street. Roughly within fifty to seventy-five yards of the car, I raised my rifle to shoulder level, held my breath for steadiness, and made a commitment.

With the silhouette of the back of her skull in my scope crosshairs, and my finger pressed anxiously on the tip of the trigger, I started negotiating the critical precision of sending a bullet to the nucleus of her cranium like a decorated American sniper would. Instantly, within nanoseconds, I had this remarkable insight to analyze the repercussion of my actions and decided to neutralize my lethal mission. I lowered my weapon to my hip and resumed my oxygen intake for a moment while I watched her vehicle vanish into the distance. I was so bothered by the visualization of the damage I could have caused during the heat of the moment that I raised my assault rifle vertically to the night sky and discharged several rounds at the twinkling stars while I screamed like an enraged commando to release the negative adrenaline. All the nerves that made up my bodily chemistry were misfiring right after each other like a Fourth of July celebration.

Disoriented, I paced around a couple of times to get my composure. After I noticed a kid resting on his bicycle watching me like he was traumatized, I made my way back inside my home, closed the garage door to Valhalla, and immediately took off the underwear that was so disrespectful.

CHAPTER 6
INDULGENCE

After my trifecta winning streak crapped out, we had a dialectical sit-down in addition to settling on a condition of total segregation, which required a posthaste departure for me to leave our home to her and the children. I disgracefully resigned my post and lowered the national flag, which only I could see, to half-mast while I listened to the melodious sound of Taps that only I could hear, for my memorial service as the self-appointed general of this once promising family. Then I retired the overzealous militant character that I shamefully personified with a figurative twenty-one gun salute.

    I was semi prepared for the culmination of this day, but I'd underestimated my love for her. I really thought that I'd be better prepared emotionally for the outcome. All I could fathom was Cat and this undesirable intruder living happily ever after, which repulsed me and burdened my solar plexus with a thousand knots like there was a signal automatically preset to constrict my abdominal region every time my heart considered the likelihood, which never seemed to quit. I felt disenfranchised and needed to put as much physical distance between us as possible, so I devised an emergency evacuation maneuver to live temporarily with my friend in his opulent lakefront home, which was remotely located in a very affluent part of the city, until I could find my own place. His royal name is Sutekh Kek Shayatin, but he strongly insists everyone call him Cowboy because his birth name is mispronounced with an unsympathetic tongue by many American challengers on our side of the western hemisphere.

After arriving at Cowboy's home, I gave him a brief rundown about my troubling relationship conundrum, and he said, "I'm going to be candid, but let me ask you in advance for forgiveness just in case there's anything I'm about to say that is offensive or appears to be insensitive, all right?"

"Okay," I allowed.

"The earth wouldn't rotate right if it wasn't for dualism, so regretfully, even adverse misfortunes we can't understand serve equally good purposes."

I was a bit confused, so I asked him to elaborate. "That sharp thorn up your ass hurts like a bitch doesn't it?" he said.

"Well, factually, I don't have anything foreign up my ass, but I am feeling some discomfort from a surplus of feces that I'm going to dump in your miniature porcelain cyclone as soon as I get comfortable and unpack."

"Man," he said, "I don't know any other person who hauls around as much shit in his colon as you do."

"Well, some mysterious character thought it was funny to curse me with irritable bowel syndrome—little did he know, it's a blessing in disguise.

"Really?"

Yeah, fecal matter is the only intimate companion that has stayed devoted with regularity, so let's say that I appreciate the frequent visits. Besides, I don't have the motivation to be too ambitious in life, and since feces are biodegradable, I can take a little pride knowing that my legacy will proliferate in the dirt for generations."

He squinted his eyes at me and said, "Why are you taking craps on the ground? What are you, a fuckin' camel?"

"All right, the metaphor I used was misrepresented. Look, it's been a long week and I'm tired, okay, but I understand that you're using analogies to make your point . . . so allegorically, I'll say yes, it does hurt."

"C'est la vie! That's a fancy way of saying, *what can go wrong will go wrong*. It's Murphy's Law in action, brother. So I guess you would like to know what the fuck you can do about it, right?"

"Enlighten me," I said.

"First, let me tell you that our kind has been trying to get it right since the beginning of time with these creatures we call women, and the world's greatest scholars still struggle with disseminating a comprehensive, permanent solution. So this simple analogy I'm about to make is a parabolic reference to your current situation; you can also apply this meme to all your future endeavors. It's the best we got so far. Now, just think back in time to when you were a child or maybe even recently with your intestinal abnormality—you know, when you thought you had a little gas in your ass, so you pushed, believing it was going to be a smoke bomb, right? But, surprisingly, you busted ass and received a mocha cappuccino that wasn't served by that pretty, little bitch from Starbucks. It didn't turn out to be what you expected, but you still washed your funky ass and carried on. The moral of this story is for you to be prepared and keep a lifetime travel supply of wet wipes, since you'll never know when you're going to have to clean up your mess . . . and believe me, it will happen, because an equal dosage of hard luck keeps the world balanced.

"That's one hell of an allegorical example," I said, "but I get your point."

"Good," he replied. "In the meantime, you need to live a little and enjoy life. I'm going to play a video for you that'll uplift your spirit."

I nodded my head and said, "Cool, let me see it."

He grabbed his television remote. "Turn around and look at the flat-screen monitor on the wall." I rotated around and saw Mark Morrison's "Return of the Mack" music video on the screen. Then, I felt a mellifluous sound caressing through my ear canal, before the repetitive, prophetic chorus enraptured me. Nostalgically galvanized by the anthem, I intrinsically embodied the spirit of the Funkadelics and boogied timeless until he faded out the lyrics to a minimum and said, "This is your comeback song, Superfly, and that's the spirit!"

I opened my eyelids with the eyes of a tiger after feeling the last morsel of sensation morphing back into my anatomical form and said, "What a rush—show me some more!"

Cowboy reached inside his desk drawer and said, "I'm going to show you more." He pulled out a silver badge and pinned it to his shirt, came closer to me, and said, "Look at what this says."

I read it out loud: "Pussy Quality Control Inspector! Man, get the fuck out of here, where in the hell did you find that, because there is no such thing. There's no limit to your imagination huh; you're like Bruce Wayne. Is there anything you don't have?"

He said, "Fuck Batman and Gotham City; my people built the greatest wonder of the world on the planet first metropolis in Egypt. King Tut didn't die." He then pointed at himself and said, "Because the motherfucker is right here—you're looking right at him!" I laughed because he was looking so serious. He then continued, "But I'm going to answer your question. There is something I don't have."

"What?" I said, playing along.

"I don't have a vagina."

I continued laughing. "But you still can have one of those. People do it all the time . . . it's called *genitalia reassignment*."

"Fuck that," Cowboy said. "I don't want my cock modified, I want them both! With all the newest gadgetry and technologies happening at the speed of light . . . don't be surprised soon when I have a robo-pussy implant built right into my inner thigh. Intercourse will be just like magic when I say 'open, sesame.'"

I laughed so hard my chest started to hurt, but then I immediately stopped laughing because the ache scared me. Cowboy expounded further. "This badge certifies me as an international connoisseur of choice pussy on the whole damn planet. If there was any good Martian pussy out there, believe me, I'd know. Brother, there's nothing that has been created in the entire universe like some good, homegrown Earth pussy, except for money. Now that's an entirely different conversation in a class of its own. The abundance of money or the lack thereof could put you and your family in a subliminal caste system in the lower echelon amongst the animals or in the upper strata with the gods. The more you have, determines the supremacy and control that you will possess over others. It's magical . . . so yes, cash is king. We have to put currency first because that's what keeps the lights on so that you can find the pussy. Could you imagine a world without it?"

"Nawl, not really," I said.

"The only other nonhuman pussy that could even come close is Peruvian caviar, which is considered the pussy of the sea. It's a delicacy of an acquired taste. If you ever get the chance to have any, don't pass up the opportunity to try it. I assure you, it'll give your body a well-deserved sexual healing worth remembering—if you can get past the taste. While you're here, I would tell you mi casa es su casa, but Miss Calico is the lady of the house, and she's a territorial, jealous bitch. But I will say mi pussy es su pussy. I'm sure you can read between the lines and figure that one out."

I laughed and said, "Bro, I thank you for the hospitality, but you are nutso!"

"You're absolutely right," he agreed, "crazy is the closest you can get to the real origin of things. But you have to be very careful delving into the mysticism of discovering the many truths of the cosmos, because you can lose it all when the sky falls. Let's say for some people . . . it can be too much to handle."

"The truth of what?" I asked.

"Have you ever felt that you were the center of the universe and all of this was arranged just for you?"

"Yeah, sort of . . . but I knew that was just a ridiculous, selfish thought."

"It's called solipsism, and here's another thing—everything you do is a reflection of your God having a humanly experience."

"Huh?"

"Your supernatural identifier!"

"What?" I said, confused.

"Creation ex nihilo is the existential quantifier; it's the etiology of our orientation in this natural phenomenon of a universe we live in. I'm talking about a strange world where darkness is not really dark, and silence is not quiet at all."

"Look, man, to be honest . . . I don't know what you're saying. This package that you're selling should've included a DVD instructional manual and laymen's subtitles on a monitor for me to understand what the hell you're talking about. But I will tell you that you're getting a little creepish right now. Are you okay?"

"I'm quite all right." he countered. "It's *you* who's not okay, and you're not aware of it." He came closer to me and studied my face like my features were an abstract art exhibit, then placed his right hand on my left shoulder and said, "I've never noticed this before, but there's something special about you. I'm sensing the spiritual aurora of your veracity will announce itself and get closely acquainted with you when all the vital elements in the universe align and synchronize with the series of events happening right now in your life. But hey, forget about this for now . . . let's have some fun!"

※※※

I'd met Cowboy through an acquaintance to use his expertise to broker and manage my stock options. He was a mathematician in the sophisticated dominion of numbers, had a niche for finding stocks with liquidity, and he could strategically execute transactions with the speed of a king cobra to maximize profits in this volatile profession. Initially, after he'd earned my trust with smaller investments, I gave him a whopping fifty thousand dollars to invest for me. With the Midas touch, he grew a substantial financial portfolio within an impressive allocated timeframe. He labored aggressive investment strategies, while loving the labyrinthian challenge of stock trend predictions, and did very well for himself making digital forecast calculation for online day trading with the New York Stock Exchange.

He was also an Egyptian national with an uncanny physical likeness to an ancient pharaoh who had been depicted inside one of the chambers of the Great Pyramid of Giza. But ironically, his heritage didn't confine him to the ancient historic customs of that region. The name Cowboy was a chosen pseudonym that he used, maybe to personally indoctrinate and endorse him into the old western culture he idolized so much.

He came from a proud wealthy family who'd made their fortune in massive commercial-development construction projects all over North Africa and several other Arabic Middle Eastern territories. He studied at Harvard University in Cambridge, Massachusetts for a degree in engineering with an understudy degree in sociology. Being an atypical successor to his father's dynasty, he dishonored his family's wishes when he was only one semester away from earning his degree and dropped out of college to become a self-made

Wall Street broker in the financial district of New York City. Within ten years of mastering the trade, he upstarted his own investment firm and relocated to Texas.

He literally loved the old Wild West lifestyle and even embodied a buckaroo persona. He lived fast and furious and personified his moniker "Cowboy" bravado with collared button-down shirts; creased jeans; handcrafted, pointy-arch designer boots that adorned costume silver-plated toe tips; and a belt buckle that was engraved with the word "Sherriff" as his ensemble signature style. Ritualistically, every morning he would first have a bump of nose candy and then simultaneously smoke a Montecristo Cuban cigar and take a shot of Louis XIII cognac, which he called "the breakfast for a champion." He also had a mantra that was his battle cry for living it up, which was, "Showtime!" And he claimed to know only two speeds: fast and faster. Characteristically, he always articulated a plethora of handpicked truisms, mottos, and slogans that he kept on reserve as a tour guide to comfort any situation and solve any conundrum of life. Most interesting though was his habit of referring to himself in the third person, saying, "This is how Cowboy does it." Cowboy had a unique pizzazz and was a very animated, eccentric type of guy who had an insatiable appetite for being the life of the party and ensuring everyone else was having a good time noticing him. However, beside his anomalous behavior and extreme enthusiasm for vices, squatting here came with tantalizing incentives and perks.

He called his megalithic domicile "Ranch Magnum," and it purposefully exhibited an architectural dreamscape, an enchanting oasis with an overabundance of luxuries and amenities to cater to any sinner's exaggerated desire. The early Spanish conquistadors of the New World in the sixteenth century would have ended their quest and declared his palatial mansion the legendary El Dorado, if they'd had the privilege of witnessing such a magnificent place. Solitude was a rarity in Cowboy's flamboyant schedule, except for the laconic time he dedicated to being alone inside his office to generate profits for his clients. With his succinct work schedule, he allocated plenteous leisure time to obsessively engross himself in insatiable successions with a voluminous group of women who occupied the west wing of his compound. This pantheon of seductresses, whom Cowboy christened as the *Thundercats,* had a libidinous appetite for the art of pleasure, with quite a few slavish talents that would make a geisha girl look like a *germaphobic* virgin. They lounged around with the scantiest accessories to cover their anatomy and were allowed in the main frame of his home only when Cowboy summoned them.

It would be categorically oxymoronic of me, in every sense of the word, to believe that having an excessive friend who lived life like there was no tomorrow would be morally supportive and understanding in my period of healing. My time of recuperating was a hoax; he was very presumptuous and definitely, an enabler who assisted in my follies by exposing and encouraging a lifestyle he practiced faithfully. In my proactive effort to adopt a replacement for my desolate, lonely heart, I found it delightful to submerge in all the decadence of leisure Cowboy candidly offered. He had the financial means that allowed him the luxury to cultivate an expensive taste and a keen talent of systematically acquiring a conglomerate of man-toys for entertainment purposes. I had the recreational pleasure of utilizing his manmade grotto swimming pool, sauna, jet skis and sports boat, motorcycles, four-wheelers, fleet of foreign cars, a billiards and game room with slot machines and a poker table, open bar, and in-house theater. His jewel on display was built into the wall of the great room—a super-size saltwater fish tank containing a deadly poisonous, translucent Medusa jellyfish. He even harbored a declawed endangered ocelot that answered to the name Miss Calico, which prowled the interior of the compound as if it was its own natural habitat.

Love Letter

One's first visit to Ranch Magnum would be tantamount to attending a Cirque du Soleil act for the first time; I found it necessarily therapeutic to abuse various gluttonous activities compulsively on a continuum basis for acquiring an oblivious awareness of my precarious circumstance. Every waking day in this man-built sanctuary, with the title of bachelor, guaranteed me a revitalized source of motivating testosterone to exploit and capitalize on my newly found entitlement of behaving as if I were undomesticated.

I had admission and the privilege to migrate freely throughout the large, multifaceted compound, with the exclusion of one room, which Cowboy simply called KV62. The border was inscribed with some unreadable ancient Egyptian hieroglyphics that bestowed a peculiar mystique. It was an unbreachable obstacle, equipped with a steel-framed door that looked like it could withstand repeated blasts from a portable rocket launcher. I heard from a dubious source that the mysterious crypt was furnished with a replica of King Tut's coffin, but Cowboy never addressed any of the circulating rumors about the anonymous contents inside or even inferred anything to give the curious mind a plausible clue. On a few occasions, I witnessed Cowboy waking up from his sleep in the middle of the night very weak and lethargic, like he suffered from some unknown sleeping disorder. His behavior was reminiscent of Clark Kent's apparent affliction in the presence of kryptonite whenever he made a feeble effort to transport himself to the chamber's door. Then, standing before a mounted high-tech security system, he'd authenticate his presence with the biometric technology that scanned his facial features and parted the sliding doors to provide him access. My curiosity always provoked me to peek, but the only thing visible from the entrance was total darkness. He would usually emerge from his infirmary within an hour, revitalized like he had consumed a powerful Superman vaccine, and then stand in front of a gigantic mirror adjacent to the entryway. Dutifully, he'd stare at his reflection with both hands close to his sides encased in imaginary holsters, as if he was stuck in a bizarre fantasy of being a gun-slinging desperado. Twitching his fingers, he'd mutter "Draw" at the carbon copy and then quickly raise his hands to shoot with his index fingers, only to blow the illusionary smoke from his digits before screeching, "Showtime!"

There was a time where Cowboy and I were inebriated as usual and headed back to Ranch Magnum from our wild, ritualistic partying at zero dark thirty in the morning. While he drove, I peered over at him to evaluate how wasted he truly was, in hopes that the alcoholic truth serum was switched to the "on" position. I noticed that he presented a hypnotic, absentminded expression on his placid mug, and a few unintended swerves of the sport car complimented my assessment of him. "How you doing over there superstar?" I asked.

Brainlessly, he intoned an inarticulate groan like Lurch on *The Addams Family* with a throaty pitch and said, "Ehhhhhhhh."

It was now or never to seize the moment with a tough interrogation approach and finally obtain classified information about KV62. Then and there, I utilized a seamless 007 technique that perfectly embodied the finesse of Roger Moore's character from *For Your Eyes Only*. I spoke with a Hollywood baritone accent for effect when I said, "So I understand that you would like to have a heart-to-heart communiqué in full detail with me right now about what's been going on inside of KV62, right?"

Because he was under the influence of some very potent substance, he kept his head forward and spoke underneath his breath. "Are you ready?"

"Confidentiality is not only my name, but it's the code of ethics that everyone here at the agency lives by," I said.

"You don't understand," he replied.

"I'm highly skilled in these delicate matters," I assured him, "so go ahead and give me a debriefing."

He nodded his head, looked at me and said, "Are you tone deaf? What I just asked your ass was: *are you stupid?* Who in the fuck do you think you are anyway—James Bond?"

"I'm sorry, I'm a little drunk," I said. I was so embarrassed that I started behaving erratically, like I was really shit-faced, to facilitate an excuse for being presumptuous about my abilities.

"Hey, bro, are you okay?"

I didn't say anything as I was busy pretending to dry-heave into my own lap to endorse the falsehood of the reason for my peculiar, inquisitive behavior.

"Buddy, you need to lay off the alcohol for a while and let your system detox, because I have never seen you like this."

After I fictitiously pulled myself together, Cowboy said, "I'll tell you what—I'm going to allow you to ask me only one inquiry about KV62, so think about it and be resolute about your question."

I was sure he could detect the excitement of my aura spilling over onto my expression when I looked at him and said, "Really?"

"Absolutely, and I give my solemn word that I will be truthful."

I thought to myself, *shit, you lucky motherfucker, you're about to get the goose to lay the golden egg.* I contemplated severely about what question to pose and then I said, "What do you do inside?"

He spoke something that I couldn't understand in his native tongue. "What does that mean?" I asked.

"Pay my dues," he said sharply.

I didn't want to appear naive about complex economics, and I wanted to say something clever so that he would believe I was also a man with a sophisticated range of abstract knowledge on a polymathic scale. I went into my mental factory and quickly manufactured a blue-chip product to demonstrate that I was a scholarly man and said, "Oh yes, don't we all. I pay mine all the time whenever I sit on the porcelain altar to drop the kids in the pool."

When the last syllable left my lips, I thought, *why in the fuck did you say something so juvenile about taking a crap? Now he knows that you're amateurishly clueless to his meaning.* Beneath his transparent smile, I think he knew my cultivated awareness was unenlightened. It was especially confirmed when he gave me a condescending pat on the shoulder and said, "In time."

While I simmered over not asking a better-suited question that was more specific, Cowboy said, "Look straight ahead. I want to show you something." He then revved up his Ferrari to 120 miles an hour and dipped into the opposite lane of the highway to play the fatal game of chicken with oncoming cars. I looked at him to discern if this was a joke or his death wish, but his eyes were indecipherable as I tried to read his intent. I noticed that somehow, without my observation, he had slipped a pair of gloves on like he was simulating a Formula 1 racing event on the Xbox 360 in the safety of his living room without any real consequences. As we engaged closer to the approaching vehicle, he reached down and turned up the volume to Tupac's song "Ambitionz Az a Ridah."

Petrified, my first reaction was to reach for the door handle and dive out of the car like a stuntman in an action movie, but I changed my mind when he asked me, "You're not scared, are you?"

My facial expression cracked a counterfeit smile while my spineless vocal cords refused to protest his reckless decision, and I fixed my mouth and dumbly said, "Never!" But unbeknownst to him, I whispered, "Oh, my goodness! This motherfucker is trying to kill us!" Then my frantic conscious attempted to alert my intelligence into action, by conveying the morbid thought of myself remembering the crash-test-dummy commercial. I thought, *oh shit this is fucked up . . . I'm not a damn mannequin . . . I'm an actual, real person!* My time was up to effectively resolve this problematic situation, because the other vehicle was only about two hundred meters from a rendezvous of mangled metals. I wanted my mama desperately, so I reached down and squeezed the gentle seat cushion that reminded me of the protection and security I felt during her third trimester of pregnancy and prepared for my lethal final destination.

Squinting my eyes and bracing my body for the anticipated severe collision, I unhappily made peace with my soon-to-be fate. Then, right before impact, the other car swerved, avoiding the head-on collision. I was instantly relieved, but the near encounter must have encouraged his ego, because he accelerated faster to 150 miles per hour into the path of another car. I thought, *I don't want to die like this*, as I felt incontinence requesting an emergency exit through the rear chute of my body, and the idea of that humiliating probability made me barter with my innards that I would do something if it promised not to discharge at that moment.

I had to think of something quantum-fast that would be persuasive, and at the same time wouldn't make me appear like a coward. I forged some exaggerated excitement and said, "Man that was cool, let me try it!"

"Okay," he said, "but after this one."

I looked ahead and watched the other vehicle flashing headlights, and I threw a tantrum with my arms flailing in the air like streamers at a child's birthday party and yelled, "It's my turn! You had yours! Why I can't have fun?"

He looked at me in disbelief, like an exasperated father glaring at his delinquent child in public when his misbehaving juvenile humiliates him. Before giving me his submission, Cowboy said, "Okay, since you going to act like a baby about it!" He veered back into the correct lane and slowed down to a stop onto the shoulder of the motorway. I was glad that I reacted like an infant, because that next vehicle was a hazardous semitrailer hauling diesel fuel. We switched seats, and I turned off the music, pretending to be disappointed and telling him that I didn't want to play anymore because the semi was supposed to be mine and he'd made me miss my opportunity.

He closed his eyes as I safely entered back onto the highway, and before he collapsed into a stuporous mien, he whispered, "I could've beat 'em—that's how Cowboy does it."

I shook my head. He was becoming an increasingly reckless endangerment to my health and welfare, so right then and there, I made it a priority to plan my exodus and find my own housing space of normality, ASAP.

One week before my anticipated move out, Cowboy invited me into his office to show me a picture on his computer. It depicted an attractive villa transfixed in the scenic, snowy winter of the Colorado Rocky Mountains, and he was about to purchase it. I was impressed and told him that he was a lucky man. He said, "Luck doesn't have anything to do with my success. It's imperative to be selective early in life, developing a passion for something that's lucrative. Wherever you are in life is your worth according to you, and everyone is getting exactly what they deserve because of their ambition or lack of it. Choices are everything."

"Damn," I said, "I wish I could start all over, because your life makes me regret a lot of decisions I've made." He told me that I didn't have to be regretful, and I could make a radical choice right now. Confused, I asked him, "What choice are you talking about?"

Cowboy disclosed to me that he was investing two hundred fifty thousand dollars of his own money, which would double in thirty days and net him a cool half million, and he said I could do the same. I was flabbergasted and asked him how. "I have a Wall Streeter insider that receives payola from me and other colleagues I network with on a routine basis," he informed me. "That payoff guarantees us a lucrative return on our investment in exchange for info; my hustle is procuring reliable information for a living."

"Wow, that's too easy," I said.

He grinned. "It could be complicated for the average person, also more work involved than what you think. There are other, subliminal facets I have to nurture just as much as the conspicuous particulars to ensure success. I just feel more comfortable securing a safeguard to protect my financial investments along with my clients." He was an unadulterated genius, virtually simplifying a complex matrix of numerals, and flipping a legitimate operation into a staged boiler room pump-and-dump scheme which he and his affiliates used surgical precision with their unconscionable method. They artificially inflated the value of stock shares and sold them to super-wealthy millionaire and billionaire investors who could afford to take losses, but he assured me that no Joe Schmoes from the working class, who made less than a million per year, were affected.

He then showed me statistics and diagrams of exponential growth expectancy within the next thirty days. He could tell that I was still hesitant and skeptical, but he convinced me, saying, "This is the American Dream—Monopoly on a global scale. The bankers to the Fortune 500 companies and all in between, including the richest families in the world, have made their riches and built their wealthy dynasties with phantom numbers pulled from the sky that are digitally transcribed into binary codes to tell us our worth. They're only imaginary numbers. I have the formula, and I'm offering you an opportunity of a lifetime. You can't lose, but you have to pay to play." He looked up and pointed at his ceiling and said, "If those little ambitious green men up there could hear me right now, they'd be knocking at my door, ready to play."

Still confused, I asked, "You have some painted dwarfs fixing your roof?"

"No," he said, "I'm talking about extraterrestrials, genius . . . you know, the smart ones with them invertible ultrasonic ears and shit!"

I laughed and said, "Oh, I don't have that ET money man; after paying my security deposit and first month's rent, I only got ten thousand dollars left inside my savings account to assist me in furnishing my new place."

"That, my friend, will net you twenty thousand dollars of tax-free money in your pocket, and if you could borrow more, you would be able to pay off the loan before incurring interest. It's too easy—come on, do the math."

It didn't take me long to say, "All right, I'm in!" Overenthusiastic, I darted down to the bank and made a withdrawal of the ten thousand from my savings and then decided to empty my checking account of two thousand dollars, leaving me with a balance of three hundred twenty-seven dollars to my name.

I returned, holding twelve thousand dollars in cash, all in one hundred-dollar bills. Cowboy saw the currency in my hand and advised me that, for my protection, it was best not to involve any paperwork of our transaction. He affirmed our deal was a standard operation procedure among insiders to avoid the legality aspect of the trade. Being repetitive, he overemphasized that this was a subterranean investment and not to discuss it with anyone. Because it could alert the Securities and Exchange Commission to his practices, jeopardizing the past, present, and future revenue of all his clients, including me.

It sounded practical, considering the risk, so I obliged and said, "Bro, you're doing me a huge favor, and I can't thank you enough. All I can tell you right now is that I'm happy to have a friend like you—I'm extremely grateful. I can't give you anything, so there's no other way to repay a person who has done so much for so many people including myself than to give you my loyalty and show you my gratitude . . . I have a lot of love for you, bro."

"Likewise," he said. "I knew I liked you for some reason, and every time I forget, you never fail to remind me."

We shook hands and shared a brief brotherly embrace. Cowboy then looked at me and said, "What do you think about doing what I do?"

"Being a stockbroker?"

"Yes."

"I don't know . . . that's not my forte."

"Come-on, you can make a ton of money . . ." he advised me.

"I don't know the intricate details of your profession. That's why I hired you, remember?"

"I can give you a crash course to simplify those numbers, and within no time, you'll be a financial predator like me."

I jolted when he made that reference. "Predator?"

"Hey, I apologize for the terminology," he replied. "That was simply a slip of the tongue. Sometimes my silver tongue gets a little carried away when speaking about money. But to be truthful, you have to be spot-on, and quick-witted with your vernacular, because conversation rules the nation."

"Why me?" I asked.

"I've realized you're someone I may be able to finally trust. You have a heart of gold that's transparent and genuine, and for me to feel this way about anyone is unusual. That's a rare human quality you hold, especially in my line of business. You know what I'm going to do?"

"What?"

"You've had a taste of what money can bring, so I'm sure by now you have an itch for the good life?"

I nodded my head and said, "Yeah."

"I've been considering making you a partial partner in my organization, which will give you a quarterly shareholders' percentage that's predicated on how well the company is doing. But I can tell you, we love to win . . . and winning is a habit. Currently, my associates and I have plans on diversifying, as well as expanding abroad to other countries, and we're going to be a major juggernaut in this international game. The financial world puts crowns on guys like us, Michael . . . and I'm going to tell you, I have an awesome brain-boner every time I make a lot of money. My life is monumental . . . if I had to go to hell to pay the price for it, I'd do it twice. Your legacy can start right now, with something tangible, and not in the fuckin' dirt okay. So tell me, are you ready for uncountable riches that will provide you endless opportunities of jet-setting across the world to live the highlife in the fast lane, motherfucker?"

I removed the wrapping from around the stack of money I was holding, threw the whole wad in the air, making it rain down big-face hundreds and said, "I'm going to feed Benjamin Franklin's pudgy ass some of Popeye's spinach until he gets green stretch marks. Then when he gets swollen and start complaining that he's full, I'm going to say, 'Shut up, and stop actin' like a little punk.' I'll keep overstuffing his fatness until the back of his lard ass explode from obesity and then I'm going to collect all those individual stretched-out pieces of that once-inflated piggy bank and do it all over again. I'm talking about money producing more money . . . so hell yeah, I'm ready to talk shit like Rick James."

Cowboy knew precisely what popularized catchphrase I was talking about when we put our arms around each other's shoulders, leaned back, and yelled, "I'm rich, bitch!"

"I knew you had it in you," Cowboy said. Then he poured two glasses of Louis XIII cognac, we lit each other's Cuban cigars to celebrate our declaration, and he said, "I'm very pleased about you coming on board to become an integral addition to this investment alliance. Later, there will be an official ceremony to induct you into our private brotherhood, known as the *Immortal Outlaws*. But first, let us prepare for a farewell pool party this upcoming weekend that will be a proper blessing from me to bid you valediction leaving Ranch Magnum and to wish you good luck with your new casa."

I said, "Man, you so fly, you got a wingspan like a pterodactyl that flew above the dinosaurs, and you don't even know it."

The following Saturday, Ronnie with his outfit of bikers muscled their custom choppers to my shindig looking like *Sons of Anarchy* bandits. Cowboy ordered *Penthouse Nymphos* on Time Warner's pay-per-view channel to be played on every flat screen monitor throughout his home to set the tone for some wild entertainment. He also ordered the bodacious Thundercats to parade around as showgirls, wearing stars-and-stripes high heels, along with matching bikinis painted on their bodies to illustrate the American flag. Some of their duties consisted of providing refreshments, showcasing their hands-free abilities to serve liquor between their breasts and to use anything necessary to titillate and satisfy the boys' animalistic nature.

During his commencement speech prior to the festivities, he pitched only one bylaw for all invitees to follow at Ranch Magnum: his infamous, uncompromising "open door policy," which granted him the lawful right of free reign to exploit the privilege of gratifying his voyeurism inside the confines of his administration.

"Attention playboys and playgirls. All that I ask is for you all to play hard, and don't forget to be generous enough to leave the doors open." Then Cowboy spread his arms as if he was Caesar and said, "Tonight, I stand as your commander-in-chief, giving you all a presidential pardon. With the USDA seal of approval, this mansion has been certified as the best little whorehouse in Texas within a thousand-mile radius, so let the games begin!"

Sometime during the jamboree, Cowboy revealed an unapologetic sign of being a sadomasochist. He appointed a few of the Thundercats to play the role of dominatrices and commanded them to abuse him into exhaustion. Shamelessly, he publicized the whole spectacle in front of everyone, like we were patrons inside a brothel at Amsterdam's red-light district. It appeared he received spikes of endorphins from every whip delivered to his flesh with an ambivalency of elevated emotions. His expression suggested that the pain hurt so good, while the bikini-painted vixens seemed to be just as equally sadistic. No one seemed to be offended by the biblical theatrics of the Sodom and Gomorra epic tale, because several people, including me, encouraged the exhibition by cheering him on.

Late in the evening, a few of us got restless and created an alliance among us to instigate a rowdy game of ganging up on one person and throwing the unlucky contestant into the aquatic hole in the ground. After some successful attempts of throwing a couple of the fellas into the water, my band of comrades turned on me and threw *me* into the swimming pool. I wasn't too happy about that and yelled, "That's a low-down, dirty shame . . . I wish all of y'all would turn into mermaid concubines on your birthday—then how tough would you look with permanent spandex and flippers, you damn whorish bikers!"

I got out of the water and went into the house to change my outfit and then I realized that my mobile phone was still inside my pocket. With optimism, I pulled it out and checked to see if it was working, but unfortunately, the device was dripping unresponsively. I was waiting for an e-mail back from the property manager of my new apartment about augmentations I wanted to make the next day, which was my scheduled move-in date. So I took the battery out and dried the contents as best as I could, but to no avail; the device was still inoperable.

With a fresh set of clothing on, I went to the unattended bar and poured myself a drink of Patron. Before I rejoined the party, I decided to sneak into Cowboy's office to use his computer, since my cellular device was a deadbeat. I tried accessing his computer, but it was locked with a password protection. So I sat down at his desk to finish up my tequila, thinking, *I'm really going to miss calling this place home, but a man needs his own space.* I reached over to the wastebasket to throw away my Styrofoam cup, and inside I saw a piece of paper that had the word "Sucker" written across it in a highlight marker, in Cowboy's handwriting. Curious, I picked it up out of the trash and noticed it was a personal letter that someone had handwritten to Cowboy.

CHAPTER 7
DISILLUSION

The content was disturbing; the author of the letter was accusing Cowboy of embezzling her family inheritance of two hundred thousand dollars. Stating that she and her husband had entrusted Cowboy to invest their life savings so that they would be able to afford the healthcare for their only child, who had been involved in a swimming accident that left the child a quadriplegic. When the couple learned of the betrayal, Cowboy denied all acknowledgements of representing the family and receiving the cash payment. Before long, the couple's meager finances couldn't afford them adequate assistance to care for their daughter, so she passed away. The father felt so guilty for trusting this so-called family friend who had come into their lives, even appointing him godfather to his daughter, that he committed suicide after the child's passing. The only living victim in that family was now trying to cope with the loss of her loved ones, and she wanted Cowboy to know how he'd single-handedly caused a great deal of destruction without any empathy. What was deeply heartfelt about the letter was the part where she stated that she had forgiven him and only wished that someday he would have enough compassion to feel remorseful about what he had done. Sadly, she'd signed her name at the bottom of the letter as *Cynthia's Broken Heart*. I couldn't believe that he'd had the audacity to write "Sucker" on top of someone's agonizing pain—which he had caused. The luridness of Cowboy's treacherousness, had to be the most heartless thing I'd ever read.

Slowly but surely, I thought about my money he'd been investing for me and got the chills. "Please don't tell me that he deceived me too!" I said out loud. I leaned forward on his desk with the shakiest hand, as if I had Parkinson's disease and grabbed the mouse to awake his computer screen. I had to bypass the password protection to get to his files, so I began entering random cyphers I believed Cowboy would use until I came down to the final attempt allowed before his computer would be temporarily locked. I paused and thought very hard what my password would be if I had a bumptious ego like Cowboy. Then I typed in "KingtutKV62" and hit enter—jackpot! But before I could rejoice, some background noises put me on edge. It sounded like a crowd of people was entering the house, so I knew I had to be expedient with my findings.

I searched through his files, looking for anything that was suspicious or indicative to any signs of skullduggerous accounting schemes. I was so overwhelmed and stupefied looking at analysis, graphs, projections, and a septillion of mind-boggling numbers entered into spreadsheets that I said, once again out loud, "What in the hell I'm looking for; I don't understand any of this shit. Damn, I'm so fuckin' stupid!" Then, while my hopeless intelligence continued to browse, I jumped out of the chair because I'd hit the big bonanza. It was all too obvious of a clue for him to be so emboldened to have a dossier titled *The 30-Day Losers Contribution Fund*. "Yes!" I said.

I accessed the file and saw numerous victims' names associated with this scam, totaling an amount that had netted him over one point two million dollars. I anxiously went through the list, looking for my name, until my search ended when my ten-and-a-half-ounce heart fell through my virginal asshole and hit the floor, shaking my whole world. I said, "No, this can't be . . . that's all I have!" After I picked up my heart and placed it back into my chest cavity, I balled my fist up and gave myself a blow to the torso, kick-starting my heart to keep myself from going unconscious. I couldn't believe that my friend and business associate had swindled me out of twelve-thousand-dollars, and I was sure to believe that I've been defrauded out of my initial fifty thousand as well. Even worse, it really takes a lowlife son of a whoremaster to victimize their guest, then throw them a hasta la vista party. I was explosively livid, wanting to accost him and beat him into a pulp, but first I needed to secure evidence of his embezzlement.

I inconspicuously stepped out of the office to see where Cowboy was, so that I could make time to get a hard copy of as many incriminating documents as I could find. I peered around the partition into the great room and saw him dancing with a lasso, roping women like they were livestock to the familiar song "I Need a Freak" by the California music artist Egyptian Lover. Looking at his sadistic foolery, I wanted to attack and beat him on-site like a piñata until he dispensed candy, but I had to keep my poise until I had the proof I needed.

I crept back into the office, locked the door, and went to work looking for more files of his corruption. Cowboy had several archives of investment earnings, and I wasn't sure of what red flags to look for that could tie him to his nefarious activities, so I just began printing everything.

Before long, there was a knock on the door and I heard Cowboy asking, "Who in the hell is copulating in my office with the door closed? You're in violation of Cowboy's open-door policy that gives me the right to arbitrate all fornicating sexcapades, and house rules will be enforced." I didn't answer because I was busy reprimanding the insubordinate copy machine, shaking it from left to right to stop procrastinating and work more expeditiously. But my attempts were futile as the defiant apparatus ignored my request and continued to spit out copies at a predesigned rate.

"Okay," Cowboy warned, "I'm going to give you two minutes, and I don't care if you're stuck like dogs, I'm coming in looking for elbows and assholes."

But he lied about the two minutes because within seconds, I could hear his key entering the keyhole, and before I knew it, he was standing inside the room with the door closed, holding his costly King Louis XIII bottle and asking me, "What the fuck are you doing? Why in the hell are you locked inside my office when everyone is out there? Get your ass out of here, and let's party like rock stars!"

"Right now, you need to curb your enthusiasm, because I didn't know you were profiteering off of people's grief so that you could live an extravagant lifestyle."

Clueless, Cowboy said, "What are you talking about, bro?"

I snatched the heartbreak letter from his desk and teleported over to him with the correspondence clinched between my fingers. I opened it up in his face and said, "*This* is what I'm talking about!"

Unperturbed about the confrontation, and with a nonchalant attitude like he was Chester Cheetah, he casually said, "So what?"

"What the fuck you mean, *so what?* You're destroying families!"

"You have a lot to learn," he said. "Being ambitious means you can't feel sorry for none of these motherfuckers."

"But you assured me that the average person won't be affected."

"Yadda, yadda, yadda . . . don't be a fuckin' simpleton. There will always be losers . . . the dumber, the better. It's the movers and shakers in this world that make things happen. The meek aren't going to inherit a goddamn thing. All the high-powered financial predators like me didn't take what we have just to give it away to a bunch of unmotivated, lazy motherfuckers. That'd be un-American of me; it's this country that taught me what being an American is all about. This is the best country on the whole planet for exploitation. We're all thieves fighting for position, from the biggest tycoon to the smallest crumb-snatcher who just got birthed, and everyone in-between. You have to take what you want by any means necessary, and it's no secret who has all the power and the guns. It'll be a bloodbath before guys like me give it up to people like that—those *peasants!* You better get your head in the game before you get left behind. There isn't any justice league coming to save the day."

"That's funny, because I could've sworn I saw my name on your Losers Contribution Fund list."

"That was before I changed my mind about you and offered you a piece of the action. If you have been paying attention in this world, you should have realized by now that money is power, and opportunity waits on no man. It's us against them, Michael, we have to adopt the Machiavellian ruthlessness to become successful in this life of ours—any means necessary. So be smart and make this next move your best move." He then placed his hand on my shoulder and said, "Look, you have nothing to worry about, all right . . . you're going to be one of us now. The intelligentsia is all interconnected, and there's only one rule: don't get caught. And we never will. So are you still with me, brother?"

I looked down to form the words the best way I could so that he would understand. "I live by a different morality; I can't get close to someone and break their heart that easily. I won't be able to look at myself nor sleep well at night."

"Well, I understand how this could be sort of an ethical shock for you," he said. "Let me ask you to reconsider before you give me that as your final answer . . . so take all the time you need, and let me know later when you're ready to come on board, all right?"

"I don't need any more time," I answered immediately. "A thousand years from now, my answer will still be the same."

"I want you to think about what you saying right now . . . so I'm going to ask you again: are you sure?"

I looked solidly and deeply into his eyes and said affirmatively, "I'm dead-eye positive!"

He shook his head and said, "I wish you didn't say that, because now we can't be brothers anymore."

"Hey, that's fine, man, just give me my investments and this will be where we part—you going your way and me going mine. Agree to disagree. No love lost."

"You don't really understand do you?" he said.

"What don't I understand?"

"That there *will* be love lost if you go your way and I go mine."

"No it won't, because we'll still share memories of the wild times we've had together."

"That's the problem!" he said more forcefully.

"How?"

"Because you will also have the memory about your little discovery today. Isn't that why you're printing out files off my computer right now, in hopes of me being incriminated and prosecuted?"

"Well, you don't have to worry about that. Most of my stuff is already packed inside my vehicle, so I'll just get the rest of my things with the money you owe me and leave."

He laughed and said, "It's not that easy."

"What are you talking about?"

"What's understood, don't need to be said—I think you know what I'm talking about."

"To be clear, how about you spell it out to me?"

"You sure?" he asked.

"Yeah."

He shook his head, got right in my face, and said, "Let's call the little chump change that you say I owe you, your luxury tax. Because living here wasn't free, so that's *my* money!"

"Now I need to ask *you* something . . . and I want *you* to really think about what you're saying right now. Are you sure?"

"Bulls-eye!" he said, exuding arrogance.

He didn't know my intentions until I reached up and grabbed him by his collar with a death grip, pulled him closer and said with a low growl, "Motherfucker, you better hope that you got all my money, or I'm going to Hulk Smash you!"

With a ridiculous, petrified expression on his face, looking like driftwood, and his extremities resembling a catatonic octopus in the mercy of my clinch, he ironically laughed and said, "Bro, you have it all wrong. I was only joking. I have your money, and I was going to give it to you in the morning before you moved out. It's all right here; I can give it to you now."

I wanted to physically assault him with extreme violence, but I felt some relief to hear that he had all the funds I'd given him, so I released him. Guardedly, I studied him as he walked over and placed the cognac on his desk. After pulling a set of keys out of his pocket, he unlocked the drawer, and then took out a metal box and sat it on top of his desk and opened it with another key. Then naturally, I became awestruck when he pulled out a huge Desert Eagle hand gun and drew down on me, saying, "Sucker, that's exactly what I got . . . all your money!"

With my adrenaline racing, I immediately panicked about what to do while I kept my poker face. The first ridiculous idea that came to mind was to tell him this was all a joke and that he was on MTV's *Punk'd*, until I remembered that he was a member of the Mensa International Society with an IQ of 170. Then I thought about telling him someone was behind him so I could make my escape when he turned around to look, but that was an immature idea also, because I'd seen it that morning when Bugs Bunny use it on Elmer Fudd while I watched the Cartoon Network. I had nothing clever to suggest that could promise me a safe passage home to my 400-thread-count sheets and my Sealy Posturepedic pillow to dream of gentle caterpillars blossoming into lovely butterflies in a bed that wasn't mine any longer.

Pointing his firearm at my center mass, Cowboy then said, "Oh, now you're civilized . . . maybe because it's no fun when the rabbit has the gun. Power tools do seem to have that effect on tough guys. I see that you have rigor mortis written all over your face like a deer in headlights, but I bet you're shaking like a scarecrow on the inside."

Fuck it, I thought, *I'm going to try to make a run for it!* I turned my head slightly toward the door to calculate my chances of making it out alive.

"Don't try it, Eastwood," he told me. "This isn't Hollywood, and you're not that fast. I'll put so many holes in you that extra-large absorbent tampons wouldn't stop the bleeding. So do yourself a favor before I pop your cherry . . . move slowly, and lock the door behind you."

I reluctantly accommodated his nonnegotiable request and wished I had a crystal ball to tell me how things were going to play themselves out. He swept his weapon in my general vicinity and said, "You're an ungrateful spy. I welcome your bum ass into my home and show you a life that you wouldn't be able to afford even if your job had a job, and this is how you thank me. There is a subliminal hierarchy in this game, and you can't see it because you're intellectually handicapped about how the real world works. The world is a business, a free enterprise built for sophisticated criminals. This is what capitalism looks like. In laymen's terms, I'm talking about world domination, where only the strong survive. You eat or you get ate, and it's great sharks like me who devour small fish like you because that's the natural order of things. I'm a tactician when it comes to economics. It's all about prosperity, security, and glory. I'll befriend anyone, just as long as they're able to enrich me with everything they once had. My charisma mesmerizes these motherfuckers like a snake charmer selling dreams. And while they're enamored with the possibility of having a little wealth and infatuated with their own greedy ambition, like a master magician, I come and take it all away because their simple asses don't deserve it. You're a witness . . . you've seen how simple it was for me to use my prowess to bedazzle you with these material things that glitter. This catch-net facade is a fatal attraction to hypnotize anyone to be envious of what I have, and I'll morph into whoever they want me to be and say whatever they want to hear, while methodically siphoning everything they got. I have absolutely no love; someone else's miscalculation is my gain. I'm a proud, coldhearted son of a bitch and I don't give a fuck! I take what I want because the universe said I can, so tell me . . . who's going to stop me?"

He slowly walked toward me as he continued. "I'm of a special kind . . . the wind blows when I move." Right at that point, I observed a breeze blow around inside the room like a cyclone, swooping up the papers that were spilling out of the printer and tossing them around like feathers. While this was still going on, Cowboy strolled up motionless, like he was on a travelator, and stopped right in front of me. Then he cocked the hammer back on his bazooka-size handgun, pointed it to my face, and said, "Welcome to space age robbery . . . I'm your host, the new Jessie James, and this is a stickup."

I closed my eyes and shook my head because the scene felt like a fantasy. When I opened my eyes, all the papers in the room were back to the way they had been. I couldn't account for why I'd had that unusual experience during that moment; I thought maybe I'd blacked out and had a spell of confabulation. Realizing that he still had his gun on the tip of my nose, I kept a reticent opinion about his braggadocious oration and again wished like hell for that crystal ball.

Suddenly, he said, "Guess what?" I gave an upward head nod as if I was saying *what's up*, but devoid of speaking. Cowboy said, "I'm what you get when there's an unstoppable force crashing into an immovable object. Unsullied, extraordinary brilliance! So where is your gratitude for being in the presence of someone like a god?"

I was disgusted by his assertion of being a deity and said, "You evil motherfucker!"

He laughed hysterically at my insult. "Thank you, but that's an understatement. Satan buys a ticket and orders popcorn when I show up. What's the difference between me and you?"

I didn't say anything. He then grabbed his crotch and said, "Balls! You know . . . cojones, testicles, gonads, nuts. That's right, all the brazen metaphors that represent the courage that you don't have. Now that I'm done terrorizing you, this is what's going to happen next, you little peon. You're going to unlock that door and skedaddle your ass out of my house, go back to that crummy life of yours, and continue living like a peasant. If you ever think about going to the authorities, you better slap yourself to get your mind right and keep pretending this never happened. Because if I bleed, that bootleg rag-tag family of yours is going to hemorrhage inside out. I've done worse to people I actually liked for less. I have assassins from here to the Himalayas that will orbit your entire family like satellites, and they hit harder than the Taliban. Believe me when I tell you this . . . they'll make it hurt! Every day that they're healthy, you better look up into the sky and thank your lucky stars, because that means I'm extending you mercy."

I started breathing heavily when he made the threat to exterminate my family. He saw how it was affecting me, and with a smirk he said, "You look like you're about to blow a piston. You don't like that, huh?"

"My daughters call you Godfather," was all I could manage to say.

He giggled briefly but instantly got serious and said, "Oh, that's the saddest story, and it breaks my tender heart. Well, fuck them and fuck you! Look at yourself. What in the hell is a man like you doing with a family you can't keep anyway? You're too pitiful to not give a fuck. Didn't they dispose of you, you damn pariah? Where's your castle, big man? That's right; you lost it to a woman who sunk your battleship. Now you're a self-righteousness, broke, gypsy drifter because you're not that bright. Hell, I fucked you over because you're blind, deaf, and dumb." Then he started laughing contemptuously and said, "You lose, so now I'm going to dismiss you with a quote from Julius Caesar by saying *Veni, vidi, vici*, which means I came, I saw, and I conquered your punk ass!" He lifted his free hand and pinched together his index finger with his thumb. "Is this how small your wingspan feels right now, butterfly?"

With hurt feelings and no reservations for my safety, and with all the strength I could subpoena, I exploded with the accuracy and the technical skill of a prizefighter with a bionic arm going for a first-round knockout punch. The room echoed a *ka-pow!* It humorously sounded like the action word in a classic comic book when I socked him right in the kisser. The gun flew out of his hand and he fell back into his desk. Quickly, I met him at his workstation of deception. With the grip of a Mighty Morphin' Power Ranger, I snagged him by the collar of his shirt as he was recovering. I thrust my leg with all the strength I had into his groin section to show him those big balls were inferior to the vicious knees of the flying butterfly.

Some point during the scuffle, I was blindsided with a southpaw when he reached across his desk, grabbing his luxury brandy bottle like a Louisville slugger baseball bat and cracked me across my face. The hit felt like a career-batting average of .298, which is outstanding for a major league professional baseball player. I was ecstatic when the melody of "The Star-Spangled Banner" began to play over the loud speakers, with me standing in the center of a very bright spotlight at the home plate. Everyone in the stadium stood to their feet, cheering because I was chosen as the only fan at the game to get a once-in-a-lifetime autograph from Hall of Fame candidate Barry Bonds.

All of a sudden I got tongue-tied and nervous being in the presence of a living legend, causing me to feel woozy and my legs to become wobbly. I just knew I had to say something while I had the opportunity, so I opened my mouth and articulated as best as

I could with a muzzily, slurred speech and said, "Mr. Bonds, I'm your biggest fan."

Barry Bonds was not sportsmanlike nor was he a gentleman, because he constricted his fist and punched me in the stomach, causing me to purge a cough which seemed to help my orientation. After recovering from my disorient state of mind, Cowboy came into my vision and said, "Really? And you're my biggest loser." I looked slightly adjacent to my left and saw the Desert Eagle lying on the floor propped up against the wall; however, his eyes followed my optical direction and noticed it a second after I did. Quickly, I launched and went for his burner before he could retrieve it, but he shadowed close on my heels while I was in stride and jumped on my back. The unexpected weight caused me to lose my balance, and we both went crashing down to the hardwood floor.

We fought horizontally on a flat surface without the assistance of our lower bodies for support, torso to torso in a desperate battle to get our hands on the tool that would guarantee either of us the advantage. He cheated and fought just as dishonorably as the ethics he lived by, biting me on my face like a coward. The pain was so excruciating, I screamed an amplified falsetto so perfect you could have heard my pitch yodeling in the Appalachian Mountains. Knocks began to flutter on the outside of the locked door in rapid succession, with someone asking, "What's going on in there?" I adjusted quickly to his grungy style of fighting and bucked him off me like a wild horse, and mounted my frame on top of him with my legs pinning his arms against the floor. I then grabbed him by the face, placed both of my hands in his mouth, and attempted to dislocate his lower mandible from his upper jaw for teething me like an infant with big crocodile teeth. I reached muscle fatigue before I was successful, and he took advantage of my strength dissipating and bit my hands. I looked up in misery, closed my eyes and groaned long and deep when I was at the pinnacle of my pain. My bellowing produced an unnatural sound wave so strong that if a school of seahorses swimming at the bottom of the Atlantic Ocean could have heard the distress signal, I'm sure they would have cried for me. That agony somehow energized me with strength from beyond the cosmos, when I was afforded the power to release myself from his inhumane jaws of death. I turned him over on his stomach so that he couldn't bite me again with his mechanical ratchet mouth and started slamming his face into the hardwood floor. With every thrust, I grunted like an angry, retarded varsity wrestler who didn't know his strength because his mother didn't put the Ritalin inside his lunch box that morning.

Breaking my developmentally challenged fury, was the congregated noise of people outside the room attempting to knock the door down. I flipped him on his back while he was in a debilitating state of defeat, grabbed the gun, and placed the muzzle on the equidistance of his forehead to blast his piggy bank out the back of his skull.

"Open your eyes and look at me," I said. "Here are sixty-two thousand reasons why you're about to die, motherfucker!"

Cowboy, exhausted and beaten into inertia, looked up at me and groggily said, "You can't kill me—I'm highly favored by a god you couldn't imagine. Try it, bitch!"

I couldn't believe the balls this guy had. As ferocious as I felt to exterminate the foul parasite, I was also struck with admiration for his brash bravery in the presence of death. But my adulation wasn't stringent enough to save him, so I gritted my teeth and tightened my wrist to prepare for the recoil from the gun blast.

All of a sudden, *wham!* The door broke open, delaying my action. Through the course of the bordering excitement filtering in from the commotion, I kept my position and chose not to take my eyes or my attention away from my target.

Then I heard my friend Ronnie's voice say to me, "Bro, please don't do it—think about your family." I envisaged my absence during the growth and development milestones as my children grew into adults, and lowered the weapon to my side. *Damn,* I thought, *I wish I knew how to commit the perfect murder so that I could feel the pleasurable satisfaction of being this motherfucker's appointed executioner.*

Out of frustration for not having the viscera to murder the disease-ridden two-legged vermin, I opened my lungs, inhaled a large volume of oxygen, and screamed with rage.

Cowboy commenced to laugh at my dissuasion and said, "I told you I'm valuable. You couldn't kill me if you had Delta Force for support, you fuckin' sissified pussy."

He was the only person at his comedy show laughing until I gripped the gun tighter and shoved the barrel into his mouth. I rattled the cask around in a three-hundred-and-sixty-degree circular motion. I desperately tried to damage every single tooth in the hopes of getting all my money's worth. After I finished his oral reconstruction, I pulled the gun out of his slick trap and slapped him across his ugly expression with the gun. Then I stood up and walked out of the room, past all the spectators gawking at me.

I walked up to the bigger-than-life vanity mirror and smashed it with his gun, since I believed the doppelganger image of himself encouraged his narcissism.

While I was heading toward the entrance of the compound to leave, Cowboy staggered out of the room grotesquely, with a bloody face like a grave-robbing ghoulish monster from Transylvania. He began sputtering out blood and shattered teeth while clapping his hands and giving me a few choice expletive words, saying, "Give the boy a prize . . . but you're still a chump and a broke-ass lame motherfucker. It's still *showtime!* This is my city and you're nothing but a guest. You better look both ways before you cross the street, and trust me when I tell you this. I'm going to fuck up your life for fun!"

I continued walking, removed the clip from the gun, and dropped the weapon in the foyer before exiting the front door.

CHAPTER 8
THERAPEUTIC JUSTICE

I drove around aimlessly like a gypsy with nowhere to go, while the contents of Cynthia's letter continued to ricochet within the borders of my cranium like an inescapable bullet. I didn't want to break hearts so I thought deeply about my greatest transgression. Being humble and performing an honest analysis of self-reflection on my character was essential for me to begin my redemption, so I continued to drive around until I was positive about what was best in life. The thought of having my family back impassioned me to place them in the epicenter of my rapture.

Looking like a punch-drunk refugee, I instinctively wandered back to the home I was expelled from as though I'd just awoken out of a fugue state of amnesia. I held my breath for luck, knocked raggedly on the door, and awaited my reception. Cat opened the door in her nightgown, and with a gasp she said, "What happened to you?"

"Is it okay for me to come in?"

She allowed me to enter maybe only out of curiosity as to why I looked like a regurgitated medium-rare entrée that had been tossed in an alley in Singapore. I sat on the sofa in the once comfortable living room that looked all too familiar and asked her for a cold beer to put on my throbbing face, which felt like a medieval ironsmith was forging metal on the surface. She brought me the bottled liquid ale that I used as a cold pack to numb the pain and also doubled its usefulness as a bitter refreshment for my palate.

I didn't want to disclose the truth about the fisticuffs with Cowboy because of the embarrassment of losing all my money. So I gave her an impromptu theatrical performance. Like a seasoned thespian on Broadway, I explained, "I was viciously attacked by Miss Calico."

"Oh my God," she said, "are you okay?"

I gave her a cockamamie story about how Cowboy's ocelot pounced on me in my sleep, and I used my hand to pry open her jaws and that's how I sustained injuries to my face and hands. She was appalled by the fabricated story and suggested that I go to the hospital and get a rabies vaccination so that I wouldn't come down with cat-scratch fever. I felt like the little wooden puppet boy Pinocchio and grabbed my nose to make sure I didn't have an extension.

Cat said, "What's wrong with your nose? Does it hurt too?"

"Nawl, it just feels funny." Then I immediately changed the subject before I dug myself a deeper hole and said, "I miss you and the children. Your prodigal man and father wants to come home." She looked at me and said that she hadn't seen or heard from me in a month, and she didn't believe that we would be able to recover from our mammoth transgressions against each other.

"Well I truly love you, and I know you love me just as strong, so do you believe our beating hearts possess something special that's worth reconditioning?"

"Yes," she said.

Thrilled, I asked her if we could start now, but she told me that it would be best if we received couples' counseling therapy before we even considered living together again. I understood her reasoning and told her that I agreed with her. I then asked if it was okay to see the children; she granted me my request with the condition of not waking them up.

Before I left to pursue lodging at an affordable hotel, I falsely told Cat that I needed to go inside the Hall of Valhalla to get my toolbox. Without her knowledge, I accessed the weapons safe and retrieved a gun to arm myself for protection.

The following week, we attended our scheduled couples' therapy symposium with Dr. Zielinski in hopes of categorizing our transgressions and receive conscionable feedback from a professional who was licensed to understand and precisely mediate the nuances for a resolution. In the lobby of the office, we sat quietly on an unattractive sofa and patiently waited while a miniature Bobby McFerrin "Don't Worry Be Happy" bobble head figurine dopily shook his head at us from the receptionist desk. My apprehension was increasing until the therapist approached us and enhanced my worries even more by sporting a "Don't Worry, Be Happy" pin-back button attached to the lapel of her suit, with a pair of vibrant yellow flip-flops with Bobby McFerrin's face all over them. After she greeted us with a chipper personality, she led us down a lengthy corridor into a consultation room.

We sat on opposite ends of a loveseat sofa, with Dr. Zielinski neighboring right in front of us in an office chair holding a ballpoint pen and pad.

"Okay," she said, "it doesn't matter who speaks first, just give me some history on your relationship."

We were both silent, but then I had a pleasant ideation of articulating how we first met. I smiled and said, "The very first time I laid eyes on her it was a stunning—"

"He cheated on me and had a baby!" I couldn't believe that simple, innocuous question had ignited an instant firestorm of angry meteorites. My Spidey senses alerted me that this polarizing, confrontational session was about to get worse, so I held my head down and closed my eyes to think of something to say in my defense. After a brief moment, I opened my eyelids and held my head up with confidence.

Looking at the counselor, I said, "That's right. I cheated and unintentionally fathered a child, but Billy Jean wasn't my lover. We only had one kid."

"Oh, my goodness—" Cat broke in. "So what, do you think you deserve an oowee cookie?"

"Hell yeah, macadamia nut . . . where is it at?"

"Jackass, I was being facetious," Cat said. "You don't get a damn cookie for cheating on your girlfriend and procreating a baby, even if it only was one child."

"Well, I was just saying . . . because, you know, some guys have done a lot worse."

"Why the necessity to cheat? What do you believe precipitated your actions to be unfaithful?" the therapist asked.

I thought for a moment about my answer and how to minimize the fallout from the typical man's legendary response without appearing to be a hypersexual maniac or being told by an asexual person that I'm also a sex addict who may need compulsive sex therapy too.

While I was determining how to structure my reply, Cat said, "Why all of a sudden you pretending to be afflicted with aphasia? That condition doesn't apply to a two-timing biped that walks around twenty-four/seven with his ding-a-ling in his hand." That idea was just absurd for her to believe that feat was even physically possible. I only imagined the impression of my ding-a-ling constantly in my hand without anyone even knowing about it, so I didn't dignify her opinion with the slightest reaction.

Dr. Zielinski gazed at me and furnished a few of those famous Groucho Marx eyebrow raises, and I presumed that was her unique way of silently expressing that she would be impartial, so I said, "Yes, I was a philandering opportunist at that time because she stopped giving me my daily allowance."

The therapist took off her glasses and offensively said, "Excuse me, but why are you a grown man who's in the need of an allowance anyway . . . do you not work?" I looked at her with disdain, and she quickly became an object of my derision when I telegraphed my facial features to her that read *you destitute, funny-looking hippie, do I look like a freeloading bum, you fucking heathen?*

Apparently, she didn't get my contemptuous transmission because she said, "It's nothing to be ashamed about. You just have to get out there and shake hands with a positive attitude while you're networking, and don't forget to paint on your happy face." I took a deep breath, as I realized that she didn't understand my choice of innuendo verbiage. She was so affable with her intention to be helpful that her insulting insinuation was pardoned. So I donated a calm face and said, "I'm sorry, the phrase I used was a double entendre; it's my euphemism for sexual satisfaction."

Cat turned to look at me and intensely said, "Satisfaction . . . where was mine when several nights a week I would ask you to stay home with me instead of going out, you selfish bastard!"

I looked at her and shouted, "You have some nerve to call me selfish, when you leased out your heart on consignment to a customer who wasn't buying—I pity the fool!"

"Michael," she said, "you need to lower your voice talking to me like that. Who in the hell do you think you are, Mr. T?"

"Shut up. He better be glad I didn't call the A-Team. Shit!"

"You're over the top with your dramatics, and that's really unnecessary," she replied.

"Unnecessary?" I said. "Let me explain the accurate diagram of that key word you just exploited." Cat rolled her eyes and turned her back to me. I felt slighted over her sign of dismissiveness, but carried on with my patronizing description. "Like deleting all my pictures off your Facebook page and unfriending me. Then, for the social network finality, you had the audacity to list your relationship status as 'complicated' so that my family, mutual friends, and the whole world could know. Now, if you're deluded about what I'm talking about, I can put it in laywomen's terms for you . . . it was unnecessarily messy."

Cat turned toward me and used the tip of her finger to assist her with speaking as if she were directing a mass choir and said, "I sure did, and I don't give a fuck!"

"Oh, okay. So you don't give a fuck, huh?"

Using that same annoying index finger to punctuate her remarks, she said, "Nope!"

Insulted, I said, "Well, maybe you should have gave a damn about what you chose to wear today, because that outfit is a little misleading."

"What?" she said.

"You should've had the scarlet letter embroidered on your chest for adulteress."

"That letter was only for married couples who commit adultery, idiot!"

"Well, there are twenty-five more letters that you can choose from to fit our situation with your smart ass. How about the letter *U* for messing around with undesirables?"

"You pompous hypocrite!" Cat retorted. "You have some nerve; maybe you should wear the letter *S* for every time I had to wash the hazelnut doo-doo stains out of your drawers with your shitty ass!"

I quickly looked at the therapist and said, "I don't know what she talking about; I ain't never *shitted* on myself."

"Psst, whatever," Cat continued, "okay, what about the dry humping?"

I was a bit confused. "Who's dry humping?"

"According to the wear-and-tear on our mattress on your side of the bed, it's you, pervert! Do you know how many nights you've woken me up with your intense grinding and moaning because you're have sex with someone in your dreams?"

"That's a lie, because I haven't had a wet dream since I was a teenager," I insisted.

She reclined back in her seat, crossed her arms, and looked away from me. "Hmph, what-the-fuck-ever!"

"Hey, your lame attempt to embarrass me isn't working, and your talking points are irrelevant. We're digressing from the reason we're here. The bottom line is . . . you weren't supposed to fall in love, the plan was designed for you to have sex with him, and that's it."

Cat promptly affixed her attention back to me. "Huh? What did you just say?"

With a quick response, I said, "Nothing." Standing up, I reached into my pocket and pulled out a folded-up mug-shot photo that I printed off the computer, and held it up.

"Um hmm, I did some private investigation work on your boy-toy, for your information. Let me tell you . . . he's no prize. This bum is a two-time felon without a real job, and he gets paid under the table for bouncing at nightclubs with no muscles. Without a doubt, this picture of the American gigolo is no lady-killer. He's nothing more than a case study. It's an anomaly for a human to have a face like an anteater; a zoologist would take great interest studying this man's behavior whenever he comes in contact with anthills. FYI, you got *Catfished!* The next time you choose to cheat, do yourself a favor by checking his background to make sure he's not a convict. And try to make sure he's got some kind of financial stability with a basic health care plan, so you don't have to be his benefactor."

I crumpled the paper into a ball before tossing it into the air like an imitative football. With the form of a professional gridiron player in the league, plus perfect timing, I punted it with a swift, theatrical kick against the wall and said, "Get the fuck out of here!"

I sat back down and gave Cat a taunting smirk because I knew she didn't have a comeback to outfox that ostentatious display of preparedness. She then casually reached into her purse and pulled out the *Busted* tabloid newspaper that lists convictions and publishes mug shots of criminals in the area. Holding it up, she calmly said, "Isn't this your pimple-faced Jezebel?"

I'd never seen her without make-up, but her facial features were all too familiar. I shrugged my shoulders and said, "I don't know, you tell me."

She snickered. "Your poker face is not convincing. But obviously, she's no cover girl, unless this magazine is doing centerfolds now on convicted prostitutes." She stood up and dangled it in my face. "That's right, your little seductress was busted selling her fruit cocktail. Now, what do you have to say about that?"

Oh shit, she's a whore—I thought she was only a stripper. I didn't reveal those lyrics verbally; I just kept eyeballing her with my poker-faced expression and remained silent.

Cat appeared irritated about my reticence. Putting her hand on her hip, she said, "So you still going to lay back and sit there all cavalier and blasé like you're Iceberg Slim after hearing your baby momma is a streetwalker?"

I crossed my legs like a metrosexual pimp and sucked my teeth for effect, and I said, "Cool as ice."

She took her hand off her hip, shook her head, and said, "This shit is unbelievable. I would've liked to give you the benefit of the doubt and say that you actually gave a fuck about this promiscuous parasite giving you a disease, but your duplicitous recklessness is very believable because you're a pathetic jackass. Now I understand why you were attracted to this asymmetrical-looking donkey. Yeah, I saw her Twitter account . . . I didn't know forest animals with hooves could type. The dizzy slut has the audacity to list her occupation as an exotic dancer—can you believe that shit? I seriously doubt that she's taking off her clothes at a strip club to pay off her college loans, because the ignorant bitch is a high school dropout."

She couldn't break me; I was ironclad with my reticence, and my discipline didn't allow me to react. My nonchalant attitude didn't deter her from her vocal assault because she continued her relentless diatribe.

"Her pictures on the Internet are atrocious—taking tragic selfies in the mirror looking like a strung-out dope fiend on skid row inside a cramped bathroom with nasty underwear scattered all over the damn floor. The next floozy you choose to stick your naked dick in, make sure she's not a felonious stripper who's also a full-time hooker. So the next time you're engaging in your proclivities, make sure you do the same and practice what you preach, you fucking hypocrite!"

She sat back down, folded her arms, and rolled her eyes at me. I uncrossed my legs and sat forward.

"Look," I told her, "their occupational hazard and criminal record doesn't matter because you didn't stick to the goddamn plan anyway."

She paused silently for a moment. "That's what I thought you said earlier—what plan are you talking about?"

Leaning back, pointing at myself with my thumbs. "Did you really believe this guy was naive? Wrong, lover girl, I watched the affair develop from its inception."

Cat said, "I don't understand. If you knew what was going on the entire time, why didn't you say anything?"

"Shit, it doesn't matter now—your heart is unrecoverable; it's no good."

She looked at me now with a genuine, unassuming curiosity and said, "Please tell me. I need to know."

After feeling her inquisitiveness was permissible, I nodded my head and then said, "Okay, I'm just going to be straight up with you. Those conversations on Facebook were staged to make it look like I was having an affair, so that you could find it."

"Why?" she said.

"I concocted this plan to provoke you to have an affair so that I could have some leverage on you when I exposed the truth about having a child that was conceived as the fruit of adultery."

Cat furiously erupted out of her seat, screaming, "You degenerate asshole! I can't believe you orchestrated this perverse plot to exploit my values! How dare you do this to me . . ."

After that moment, all I heard was; blah, blah, blah-blah, blah. My attention blurred as I looked off into another direction and went tone deaf. I wonderfully drifted into another calmative period of time when our relationship was filled with bliss and imagined us holding hands with jovial smiles on our faces, skipping through a field of dandelions. Then the buds of the flowers begun to break away like little parachutes in the wind, causing a blizzard of white blossoms to overwhelm us. In the flowering onslaught, I panicked and thought, *oh shit, this is not Never Never Land!* I let go of Cat's grip and started running through this pasture of never-ending dandelions, until the pollen thrust into my nostrils caused me to discharge a rapid succession of sneezes that broke my frightening spell.

When I snapped back and awoke from the daydream, Cat was still going on and on about me being the prince of her darkness. I intently looked at the therapist, awaiting her involvement; however, I noticed that she appeared to be enjoying our turmoil. Because her face was lit up with delight, as if we were a couple of virtuoso thespians on a grand stage putting on the magnum opus of our lifetime directed by the world-renowned Shakespeare. I imagined her applauding and jumping to her feet to give us a standing ovation, saying, "Bravo! Bravo! Bravo!" and requesting an encore.

I jumped up and clapped my hands in her face and said, "Hey, lady! Why are you smiling, and what kind of bootleg practice is this, anyway, that will allow you to show up at work wearing happy feet flip-flops? Is this a funny joke?"

"Sir, absolutely not," she replied. "This is Exhale Therapy, and I will agree that we are unorthodox, but our process is considered "venting" psychotherapy. The objective is reaching closure by allowing our couples to express their anger with one another, which should explain the soundproofed, padded walls. I'm here to arbitrate and to guide the session with little interference as possible."

Cat was in disarray at this point and sobbing uncontrollably. I shook my head with disapproval and told the therapist, "Well, your 'arbitration guidance' is not effective. Look at this mess—it's a damn nightmare! How do I fix this?"

"There is a lot of passion in this room," she said. "I need you to channel it and use it to your advantage."

"How in the hell am I supposed to do that?" I asked.

"Try to relax and concentrate on the affection you have for her by digging deep, encapsulate the deepest emotional connection you have for her, and then release it, tell her how you feel. But, most importantly, express what you want as passionately as you can."

I regrouped and composed my feelings before I addressed Cat. Sincerely, I told her, "I knew that one day you would find out one way or another, because this type of betrayal is impossible to keep a secret forever. I needed you to give me infidelity as collateral to bargain with, so I contrived that scenario in hopes of you retaliating. Like a fool, I intentionally wanted you to have a sexual encounter with this guy to give me the platform, and the courage, to disclose this very painful truth. I know it was selfish, but I truly believed that I had to keep the secret concealed as long as I could, because that was my only guarantee of keeping you. I've been afraid of us getting married because I knew that a divorce was only a secret away. With a disclosure of this type of disloyalty, I figured you would be too hurt to go on, and too ashamed to stay. I'm not sure if you love me enough to forgive me for this extreme act of infidelity. But right now, I can honestly say . . . each breath of air I take is enough oxygen for my heart to love you unconditionally for a thousand years. I'll forever be your most faithful Romeo, so if the feeling is mutual, take my hand and be my most faithful Juliet."

She lifted her head while accepting my hand, and looked deeply into my eyes. "Could you promise me that you'll never hurt me again?"

With profound sincerity, I said, "Cross my heart and hope to die."

Cat then embraced me with an endearing hug and whispered, "I only did that to get your attention by making you jealous, silly." Then she released her hug and satisfied my request with an enthusiastic reply. "Of course I'll be your Juliet."

I glanced over at the therapist to thank her and noticed she was wiping away her tears. "That was aesthetic; I could only wish that all of my sessions have a similar, poetic happy ending."

We both acknowledged her sentiment with a thank you, and we affirmed our love for one another with a kiss on the lips. The therapist told us that she had a souvenir to give us as a token for our breakthrough; she stood up and walked over to a vertical cabinet, pulled out a pair of Bobby McFerrin flip-flops, and handed them to us. I told her that I would always cherish them in remembrance of this day.

CHAPTER 9
QUIXOTIC AMBITION

Life was good. My structural bond with Cat was stronger than a citadel fighting off invading forces of savage Vikings, and we were content spending more quality time with each other than a pair of inseparable booty cheeks. Our picturesque family had begun indulging in many pleasurable outings to confirm for our children that their mother and father's con amore was the leviathan among all the charming love tales that they'd ever heard. With the re-mastering of our passionate, burning desire for one another, eternal happiness seemed inevitable, and we were certainly headed for hedonistic glory.

Cat once told me that her dream birthday would be vacationing in Barcelona, Spain, if she weren't so afraid of aeronautical machines, so I decided to make her dreamscape a reality. Consequently, I took a proactive step toward eradicating her hyperbolic fear of flying by scheduling us a preliminary helicopter flight excursion. Then, arrogantly, I contacted a travel agent and booked an all-inclusive vacation for her next birthday.

On the day of the test flight, we had reservations to eat at an exquisite gourmet restaurant called Epicurious that's located on the top floor of a premium hotel in the city. It's a haute eatery with the most elegant furnishings and interior decorations that I've ever seen arranged in a single location. The establishment elected not to provide menus or divulge its prices; ipso facto, I believe it gave them an exclusive appeal to their high-end clientele. However, unbeknownst to Cat, the helicopter company that I booked for us was located on the rooftop of the skyscraper, awaiting our appointment.

I was looking dapper in my début appearance as Sir Michael, and I opened up the scene with the rolling credits of a purple fedora to fit over my braincase. Continuing the sequence for maximum exposure, I adopted the aristocratic cashmere black-and-white hounds-tooth-patterned scarf, which courted the silky purple shirt that embraced my torso. To cover my bipod, I elected to wear a pair of salt-and-pepper puppy-tooth fabric slacks perpendicular to a purple pair of exotic Belvedere Milan Stingray/Eel shoes, which complimented my every step. Lady Catharine, whom I would like to believe was presented as a debutante glitterati, corresponded the hue with a scrumptious, form-fitting pomegranate Giorgio Armani dress, along with a pair of raspberry-colored Chanel pumps. She also incorporated some elaborate, temporary empurpling body art that was freehanded earlier at a local day spa on her neckline, which paid a generous tribute to the cleavage and synchronized the feng shui of her inner self. Our apparel was meticulously coordinated, because we had chosen to name our date *The Purple Rain Challenge*. After we were greeted, we sat down and made small talk over our succulent appetizer of organic fresh fruit served with artisanal chocolates grown in the Amazon jungle. While I was fixated on having intercourse with my produce, Cat distracted my attention with her infatuation of the restaurant centerpiece hanging from the ceiling and said, "Michael look at that beautiful chandelier."

I glanced at it and said, "Yeah, I saw it when we first walked in . . . it's nice."

"Guess what it reminds me of?"

"What? The diamond head of my penis?"

"You sick—I think you should go see a psychologist for that disorder you have."

"The only thing that's out of order right now," I told her, "is that you're not undressed and sitting on this dish prepared for me to orally molest your clitoris . . . so can a psychologist fix that?"

She gave me a curious look and said, "Challenge."

I attempted to get up from my seat, when she blushed and began to gently tap the table that signified forfeiture by surrendering in the private challenge game that we began. Then she whispered, "I can't take you anywhere. You're so bad."

I attempted to give her a subliminal wink to spellbind her with a commandment to do as I please, but my novice stage as a great hypnotist was quickly recognized as a miscalculated dud when she didn't reciprocate my gesture and said, "I do believe I just tapped."

I was ashamed and disappointed that my natural, persuasive Grigori Rasputin mystical powers weren't appreciated, so I lowered my eminence to a commoner for the time being and said, "Oblige me. What does it remind you of?"

"My chandelier that's suspended fancifully in our living room. If I can recall, somebody was supposed to have it fixed a long time ago," she said.

"Oh, yeah, but I've already had two independent certified electricians look at it, and they both told me the exact same thing."

"Which was what?"

"Suggested replacing it, because it's fried."

Cat closed her eyes like she was mournful. "No, not my delicate objet d'art." Then she peered at me with pouting lips and said, "So, there's nothing that could be done?"

"No, unfortunately. They even tested the connectivity of the electrical connection from the junction box with their little gizmo to make sure . . . I'm sorry, babe."

"Well, in the meantime," she said, "can you please get rid of that antiquated mirror that I'm forced to look at and replace it with something more contemporary and hospitable with our interior décor?" Then she grabbed herself and shivered. "I swear I get goose bumps every time I look at myself in that eerie thing."

"But I adore that mirror," I said. "It's a precious, ancient artifact and should be appreciated."

"Ancient it is," she agreed. "But art—I say for a fact it's not! What's so special about that thing anyway?"

I pondered for a moment to conjure up a satisfying answer for her question and then said, "I don't know. All I can say is it has an amazing quality that's difficult for me to describe."

"You mean like a *je ne sais quoi* effect?"

"Exactly! Babe, you can replace anything else inside the home you like, but that mirror is not going anywhere. It's the only material thing in the house that I can truly say I enjoy looking at every day." She gave me a gruff look, and I realized my blunder and continued, "Well, you know, other than looking at you, that is."

She gave me a pensive expression without words, but instead of being argumentative about the irreplaceable nineteenth-century Victorian mirror, she sat back in her chair and said, "Challenge—and you better not tap out!"

Fortuitously, I was saved by the bell when the waitress ushered in our specialized entrée. Chosen by the head chef, ours were the most amazing, exotic dishes that dispersed aromatics into our nostrils like nose porn. We then engorged our palates with the gastronomy of mouthwatering pleasures that gave our mouths an orgasmic rush. The meticulous cuisine was prepared by a Peruvian gourmet chef extraordinaire name Pierre who was also the restaurateur of the establishment.

We both left one peculiar-looking item on our plates. Cat asked me, "So, what do you think this is?"

"I'm not sure, but I'm not about to find out." I said.

"Hey, it can't be that bad. Everything else was absolutely delicious."

"Okay," I said. "Well, you go first—challenge."

Cat placed the strange-looking item on her spoon and eased it into her mouth but quickly spit it back onto her utensil and said, "It tastes like caca!"

I started to laugh but saw the chef and said, "Cat, hurry up and put it back in your mouth, here comes the chef."

He walked up and touched my right shoulder, and with a heavy accent, he said, "I always like to thank our first-time guests for visiting my restaurant, especially someone who knows how to appreciate a fine cuisine."

"Thank you," I said.

Cat was nodding her head because she couldn't speak. She hilariously had the unpleasant substance in her mouth, trying her best to swallow it. I was tickled on the inside, when he said, "Now, that's a fine lady who understands finishing a cook's meal is the optimal sign of approval." He then pointed at my plate and asked me, "So, you don't like the rarefied eggs?"

I said, "Of course I do." I picked up my tableware and scooped up the spectacle with my utensil, placed it in my mouth, and started chewing. I thought to myself that Cat was right—it *did* taste like shit. It was God-awful as it slithered down my throat . . . just horrible. I felt like I was being chastised or blackmailed as I falsely nodded my head to shamefully accept the same sentimentality he vocally issued to Cat.

He tapped my shoulder and said, "I'm grateful to have you here. Please come back." He continued his walk around to greet others who had also appeared for the first time at the establishment. When he was out of range, Cat said, "That was unbelievable!"

After our grand quixotic dinner, the waitress ushered in a delectable his and hers *Crema Volteada* sweet course for dessert, also selected by Chef Pierre. After receiving our optical approval for the *sugarlicious* treat, she asked me if I was ready to close out our account. I informed her that I was, and handed her my credit card before she left the table. Approximately five minutes later, the confectioning effect of the dessert had set off a rapid-fire succession of endorphins, which made me feel like I was on top of the world; I said, "Damn, babe, do you feel that?"

"I thought it was just me," she said. "You're feeling something too?"

"Hell, yeah. So you know what this means?"

She put her spoon down, gave me a kittenish grin, and said, "Appease my curiosity."

I looked around with caution, then fixated my 20/20 vision back on her gorgeous visage and said, "Right here?"

"Please."

With no inhibition, I said, "You have just cut the red ribbon for the grand opening of the Kama Sutra Olympics, so, track star, you better lace up your Nikes, because you're going to get a major athletic endorsement tonight. I'm talking about some major broadcasting—prime time!"

She bit her bottom lip, and started winding her body like a snake, and said in a melodious voice, "'*Surfboard! Surfboard! Graining on that wood, graining, graining on that wood. I'm swerving on that, swerving, swerving on that big body. Been serving all this, swerve, surfing all of this good, good.*'"

I said, "Hold up, was that Beyoncé?"

"Yes!"

"Ooh, you're so bad."

Cat gave me an ultra-sincere look and said, "I love you, baby."

"How much?" I said.

She picked up her knife and said, "Enough to bury a dead body for you."

"Damn, girl, that's so gangsta . . . I like it."

"If you like it, I love it."

"I'm sorry," I said, "but I'm not going to be able to protect your virtue if you keep talking tough like that; I'll be forced to give you this Roc-A-Fella."

"Say my name, say my name," Cat said, teasing.

"Before tonight is over, we might end up producing another destiny child and name her Erotica Blue Ivy."

"I may be young," she said, "but I'm ready . . . and you can get it."

"Girl, do you know how long it will take for me to put all of this inside of that?"

"Well, I'll give you a head start." Then she leaned forward and said, "So what you waiting for? Don't be making promises you can't keep."

"Don't tempt me, sweetheart, I'll pretend these people are not here and give you a hard-knock life."

She resumed her posture in her chair. "I'm not scared. I'll have you singing that song by Debarge."

"Which track?"

"The one that goes, *'Ooh, Ooh, and I like it.'*"

"I got the extended version memorized," I told her.

"I didn't know there was an extended version to that song."

"Yep, it's chopped and screwed too."

"Really?" she said.

"Um-hmm, I composed it." Then I began to sing. "'*You send chills up my spine every time, every time, every time I take one look at you—*'"

Cat cut me off and said, "Mmm, boy, you better quit. You're about to make me cum without touching me, and you know when it starts I'm not going to be able to stop this Aquafina roll-tide."

I gave her a seductive look and picked up a strawberry, bit it, and said, "Challenge."

With her hands planted on the table, her eyes began to roll before they closed, and then she threw her head back and moaned sensually like she was having an envious wet dream. Like a getaway driver gone in sixty seconds, her accelerated, un-rhythmic chorus reverberated into a full-blown orgasm. Our waitress walked up during the zenith of our salacious encounter and said, "Slow down, little red corvettes!"

Cat slowly descended from her climax, opened her eyes, and said, "Whoa, that was electrifying. It felt like *The Purple Tsunami Challenge*." She looked around and noticed several diners observing her. Feeling discomfited, she held her head down and said, "I'm sorry; I don't understand how that just happened. I guess we forgot where we were at and just got too carried away with our risqué behavior. I'm so embarrassed."

The waitress said, "You don't have to be; it happens here more than you think. But this is the first time anyone has ever been all the way, and from the looks of it, you have attracted some voyeurism." We both looked at each other funny after she mentioned the frequency of this sexualizing experience.

Then I looked down at my plate and said, "What do y'all have spiked into this dessert . . . crack?"

"It wasn't that," she said. "It's the caviar."

"Oh, that funny-looking dish we ate earlier was caviar?" I asked.

"Yes, it's a Peruvian aphrodisiac."

"That's why our sexual parts were activated. This place is a porno set—I hope y'all weren't recording this!"

"We do have a few discreet cameras located throughout the restaurant viewable for security matters only. So, it's not going viral on the Internet okay; your cinematic performance is safe with us."

After we were assured by our host that our sex tape would remain in the vault of the establishment, she handed me my credit card, along with a copy of the receipt and told us to have a great day. My arousal was assassinated when I glanced at the amount: the total was $628.25 for just the two of us. My body heat increased. *This dinner was equivalent to a full month's grocery bill for our entire family, or I could've paid for a whole village in Cambodia to eat top-shelf noodles for fifteen consecutive months,* I thought. *Did they really have to insult me by charging an extra twenty-five cents—what the hell is the quarter about?*

Cat interrupted my sudden heat wave and said, "Baby, are you okay? Does the food have you feeling indisposed right now? I know when you have the bubble guts. The outside of your nose beads with sweat and you squirm in your chair—exactly what you're doing now."

"Nawl," I said, "the food was great and I'm fine. I was just thinking about how to tell you about what else fantastical I have lined up for you this evening."

"Oh, really . . . I must be doing something right."

I pointed at her and said, "Yes you are, and what I have in store for you is mind-blowing." I snapped my fingers to emphasize my last statement for effect.

"Ooh la la—I can't wait." she said and gave me a joyous smile.

As we got up from the dinner table and walked toward the elevator, I thought, *that's what I get for coming inside this high-class restaurant like we're heirs from a line of blue-blooded royalty; I should've improvised this portion of the evening and pulled into the drive-through at a remodeled Burger King. Any food will make a turd.*

We got inside the elevator and Cat said, "If our waitress had taken that out of the package, it would've been hard for her to put that cargo back in."

"What are you talking about?" I said.

"Her ass! Did you see her booty?"

I thought, *this must be a trick question.* There didn't appear to be a right answer to propose, so I took the lesser of the two choices and said, "No, I can't say that I did."

"Michael, you don't have to lie. How in the hell are you going to miss all that meatloaf walking around with a pair of legs? That was a huge payload she was hauling. Her torque has to be about the same as an F-650 Ford Turbo Diesel engine. But let me tell you . . . an ass like that can't be ecofriendly. It's only good for holding a lot of bad gas, and I'm not talking about the kind you pump at Texaco. You better be glad I don't have a Nicki Minaj booty; you wouldn't enjoy the odor that's produced from something like that. It's toxic and very flammable."

I felt uncomfortable talking about another woman's anatomy to Cat, who clearly didn't fit in with the idiosyncratic nature of the male chauvinist hound dog club, so I took a topic detour and said, "Hey, are you ready for your surprise for this evening?"

"Of course I am, honey," she replied.

"Wait until you get a load of this." I said and pressed the button for the rooftop floor.

Cat got presumptuous and said, "Oh my God, don't tell me you have an orchestra up there waiting on us?"

"An orchestra maybe second best to this occasion, babe."

After that statement, she became ultra-excited and started jumping up and down. She grabbed my face before pressing her lips against mine and said, "Haven't you been the most chivalrous gentleman today."

I grinned as our ascension reached the top level and the elevator doors opened. Cat looked at the helicopter. Immediately, her exuberant smile turned into an emoji frown, and she turned to me and said, "Why is that thing right there?" I only nodded.

"No!" she said. "That's a helicopter with propellers that go around and around. I'm not doing it, and you can't make me. I want to go home."

I grabbed her hand and said, "Cat, it's time."

She snatched her hand away, placed it on her hip and said, "Michael, you know my fear of flying. You better get your money back if you already paid for this stunt!"

"Well," I said, "I'm looking at losing a lot of more money than this test flight if you don't conquer your fear right now."

She asked me to explain what I was talking about. I then told her about the first-class Barcelona birthday vacation package I had planned for us, along with the nonrefundable payment of at least half down as a retainer to secure our dates. I even explained that I would take a financial loss of an additional fifteen percent, in the event of breaching the contract if we renege. She was still reluctant, so I offered to make a deal with her. I told her if she would complete the flight, even if she decided never to get on another one, I would have a fresh box of Ferrero Rocher chocolates every morning for her.

She got bug-eyed and said, "Oh, that's my favorite . . . you wrong. You know for a fact that I'm a chocoholic fiend for those." She stood there as if she was giving it some thought and asked, "You going to be my pusher man?"

"I'll be your Willie Wonka," I told her.

"Okay. If I die, I'm going to be mad at you. Give me our last kiss."

I laughed, and we met lips.

Cat gripped my arm like a timid baby sloth hugging a tree trunk while a safety guide escorted us toward the launch pad. After we were assisted into the craft, the pilot informed us to secure our seat belts.

Before takeoff, Cat said, "This is crazy; I can't believe I'm doing this for chocolates."

The propellers begun to turn rapidly, and within no time, we ascended into midair. The heavy metal danced effortlessly in flight like a dexterous ballerina proficient in the art of ballet. At one point during the flight, Cat felt relaxed enough to look out the window at nature's collaborative wonder between the man-made structures and the natural landscape that complemented each other. The pilot illustrated a majestic tour, hovering over many historic landmarks of the city for us to sightsee, and provided a brief, informative oration about the history of a few monuments.

About an hour into the flight, while Cat was looking out of the window on her side of the aircraft, I said, "So, if a chocolate rock could get you to do something so hazardous, I wonder what a four-karat rock will get you to do."

She turned around and looked at the diamond ring I was holding and then placed her hand over her mouth and gasped as though the impression had taken her breath away.

I took the opportunity. "I love you deeply, baby. So, will you marry me?"

She moved her hand from her mouth, grabbed her head, and said, "I don't feel good."

I asked her what was wrong. She looked lightheaded and then she said, "I'm feeling a sense of déjà vu right now. Something is not right; I think we're too high. The elevation got me dizzy, and I believe I'm hallucinating."

I said, "If you think this could be *Fairytopia* right now, let's take advantage of the opportunity, and write a beautiful ending, because we're tailor-made for each other. Let's hallucinate together for the rest of our life."

She removed her hand from her head, looked at me with tears in her eyes, and said, "Do you know how many Rochers this is going to cost you?"

"Not enough." I said.

She hugged me tightly and said, "Yes, I'm especially yours. Thank you for completing me and making me happy . . . my mind is blown."

I opened a compartment inside the helicopter, reached inside, and pulled out a box of delectable chocolates with a bouquet of deep-purple roses that signify the language of enduring love. I then popped a bottle of champagne that I'd prearranged to be inside the cabin of the aircraft as well, and I said, "Now you can déjà vu with this affair marking the quixotic beginnings of our very first day."

We kissed and then toasted to a new day above the city lights that illuminated heavenly against the closing night.

CHAPTER 10
KISS OF DEATH

One bittersweet Sunday in November, I retreated into Valhalla to watch our barbaric, contemporary version of the contact sport that was idolized by the ancient Roman civilization: twenty-two of our modern gladiators playing the great game of American football on top of a turf enclosed in an edifice we call an amphitheater, televised and broadcast on the world stage of technological ingenuity, for the glory to be shared among all its fandom.

While I was on my tippy toes and gyrating to a celebratory touchdown for "America's Team," Cat interrupted my pelvic thrust by barging inside to tell me that Jackie was there to see me. Jackie came inside and sat down, and was immediately greeted with a cold, obligatory beer. Since the invention of ale, men were evolved to offer this substance as a necessary bonding tool. Before ale, our Stone Age counterparts used women as a hospitable offering to their male guests, so our modern-day women should be proud to sponsor the message of more beer. Even the presidential leader of the free world, Barrack Obama, has acknowledged the strength of what a good beer can accomplish in his much-publicized "Beer summit" address at the White House, which serves as diplomatic proof that traditionally, beer still remains a class act for all of mankind.

Jackie said, "Man, your fiancé still looks like she's floating on air since that helicopter ride. That heavy karat may be the only thing that's keeping her grounded."

"The jeweler told me I was paying a hefty price to keep her anchored," I told him.

"Now you need to get four karats for the other hand to balance her walk before she grows a hunch back and starts walking in circles."

I laughed, and he continued, "It's not hard to see that y'all have new attitudes . . . the reinvention of Mary Poppins and Mr. Rogers. Bro, your family is the real Cosby's."

"So is that good or bad?"

"Bro, that's a beautiful thing. I'm envious and I feel nostalgic for your happiness. Have you ever felt like this before in your life?"

I thought about it for a moment, shook my head, and said, "Never."

Sitting on the edge of his seat, he put his beer on the floor and placed his hands together. Then in a solemn manner, he said, "This epochal period in time right here and right now is your climax. Cherish and appreciate it. A euphoric moment like this, should be very special; it's like a precious metal, more valuable than gold. Pirates know when you have it, and they will take it, so enjoy it while you can."

I was confused why he would say these things with a fear-provoking overtone, so I asked him if everything was okay. He sat back in his seat, and with a crackling, melancholy voice, he said, "Bro, my life is so screwed up right now, even if I had a compass, I couldn't tell you which way is up. My equilibrium is dysfunctional and volatile, like a tidal wave in the Pacific Ocean."

"Tell me what's wrong," I said.

He told me right then was not a good time and asked me for a twenty-five hundred dollar loan. I told him that I didn't have that much because most of my available funds were already devoted to our European travels to Barcelona in two weeks, but I offered him what I could, which was a thousand dollars. He then thanked me and left.

One week later, Jackie called me and asked me if my family was home. I told him that Cat and the girls were out on a Candy Crush girls' retreat getting facials, along with manicures and pedicures, and may not be back for a couple of hours. He told me that he needed to talk to me and was coming over.

When he arrived, I welcomed him in, strolled over to the dinette table, and sat down while he stood awkwardly in front of my nineteenth-century Victorian mirror and stared at himself without moving a muscle. I knew that something was amiss, so I didn't interrupt his meditative state.

But after an extended amount of time, I attempted to lighten the mood with a joke and said, "It don't matter how long you stare at yourself, you still going to be *ugly*."

As if I had said the magic word, he blinked his eyes and snapped out of his paralyzed state and blurted, "What?"

"What do you mean, *what*? Get your ass over here. You been googly-eyeing yourself in the mirror for about five minutes."

He then jilted his pretty boy gaze and turned around and said, "It only took me a second to look myself over."

I said, "Bro, unless you just came down with a sudden case of narcolepsy without your knowledge for the past quintuple minutes, I don't know what to tell you."

He walked to the table and said, "Man, you trippin'!"

After he settled in his seat, I asked, "So what's been going on?"

He looked at me, although his eyes wasn't really attentive. "My problems right now is astronomical . . . the world's leading mathematician wouldn't be able to find an algorithm to put it into context."

"There's not a problem in this world too big to work out." I said.

"You think so?"

"What's wrong?" I implored.

"Lynda left me, bro." I was stunned and asked him to elaborate. "Our entire relationship has been dysfunctional ever since I lost my contracting job three months ago. Everything that could go wrong, went wrong."

"So she left you because you lost your job?"

"That's the whole reason why I asked to borrow money from you. We received an eviction notice because we were behind on our rent, but the money that I borrowed from you and my sister still wasn't enough to cover all our expenses."

"Damn," I said, "have you been looking for work?"

"The only employment I've been able to find is making ten dollars an hour, and I have to commute a hundred and twenty miles round-trip every day to get a check that will only cover the fuel to make it to work. I've built my modest empire on the security of consistently making a hundred and thirty thousand per year; I can't maintain these responsibilities and support my family on minimum wage."

"Man, I certainly understand. Was Lynda working before she left?"

"No, she wasn't working either. All the good-paying salary jobs in the area that she's qualified for are already taken, and she was repeatedly overlooked on menial jobs because she's overqualified to be hired."

I took a moment to contemplate the matter, told him I thought that there was more to the story, and I didn't believe that his life mate would leave him over finances. He told me that Lynda had written him a "Dear John" letter. He stood up, reached into his back pocket, pulled out a piece of paper and handed it to me, and then sat back down. I read the full content of the letter before I expressed my outlook about the situation.

"Jackie, she didn't leave you because you're broke. She stated in this letter that y'alls financial situation and the eviction doesn't have anything to do with it—living with you just became too unbearable. She explains that your increasing, agonizing paranoia about her messing around made her very concerned about your mental stability. She even says, because of your enraging separation anxiety, you've threatened to annihilate her if she ever attempts to leave. Jackie, she's terrified of you."

He got angry, stood up, and said, "That's bullshit, and she knows it! It's the money, man, it's the money! It's all about the money!" He went silent for a moment, began pacing the floor, and then snapped out of his deep thought and said, "If that's what she wants, that's what I'm going to give her. I know what I have to do."

"What?"

"I'm going to take it!"

"What are you talking about?"

"You know damn well what I'm talking about," he said. "Who got all the money? The fuckin' banks, man—those fat, greedy, blood-sucking bastards is the reason why this economy is the way it is. I need it right now, so fuck 'em! I'm going to terrorize this city, and no one better get in my way. All I need is five hundred thousand dollars, and then we'll move to Spain or somewhere in the Virgin Islands and start our new lives together."

I accessed my calculator on my phone, crunched some numbers, and said, "Last year, I was looking at *The F.B.I. Files* on TV, and they aired an episode about bank robberies, and an agent said that statistically, the average take on a bank robbery is roughly four thousand dollars. That means you'll have to rob a hundred and twenty-five banks to reach your half-a-million-dollar financial goal. I'm no rocket scientist, but the probability on you achieving that objective isn't in your favor."

He said, "I don't care if I have to rob a hundred and twenty-five *thousand* banks, they're going to give me that money or a lot of people are going to die!"

"Jackie, look, your extreme desperation is causing you to think irrationally right now. I'm sure you don't want to hurt anyone. If you decide to do this and someone gets hurt doing what's right trying to stop you, you will be destroying someone else's life and break up their family because you're having a bad day. Think of the damage you'll cause trying to fix a temporary problem with a malicious, permanent solution. And there is still no guarantee that Lynda will come back."

"You right." he conceded. "Fuck, so what do I do?"

"You move in with us, and efficiently use this downtime to recalibrate your life and get it back on track."

"I'm not sure if that will work."

"Of course it'll work." I told him.

"Well, you said there is no guarantee that she'll come back, no matter what I do."

"Look, before you can be good for someone else, first you need to be a better person for yourself."

"What kind of quality of life is there in being alone?" he said.

"You still have your daughter—she's your family, regardless of the outcome with your wife. If you focus on Jalyn, you'll be okay."

He took a moment to think about what I said. Then he began to sob and said, "Michael, you don't understand how much Lynda means to me and how deeply I love her. She takes good care of me and nourishes me well with affection. She's a very caring, beautiful woman . . . she's the best! I swear, I've never met anyone like her. There will be no family if she's not in the picture. I can't live without her. She has to come back. That's my baby, and I need her!"

"Hey," I said, "it's only been a week since y'all been separated; give her some more time to miss you. It's possible that she may come back after all the smoke clears, missing you just as much as you're missing her right now."

"What we had was royal, and now the most beautiful thing about my heart is missing, and the world's leading surgeon can't put it back together. Every day feels like a million years of separation between us, and the distance is growing greater and greater. My life is empty and meaningless without her. I feel dead inside because I know she's never coming back . . . our time has expired."

"I'm going to give you some advice: don't ever trust the happiness that love offers. Love may be forever, but happiness is the culprit that will betray you. Chase it, but never allow yourself to catch it, because the treachery that traitor delivers is too painful to hold once you have it. I know now that love is pain, and it was never designed to make me truly happy, but I could've never imagined it would hurt like this."

He stood up, still shedding tears, and powerfully said, "You don't treat someone who has nothing to lose like this! I'm going to show her a nightmare and make her pay for what she done to me!"

I was quiet because I was stupefied, and he walked toward the front door while I attempted to trail his footsteps soundlessly. When my clumsy Bobby McFerrin flip-flops smacked the bottom of my foot, he turned, and said to me, "Bro, a woman knowing your weakness is a grave, detrimental mistake. It's a prelude, inviting in the kiss of death. I'm going to tell you the greatest paradox about life . . . it could take you a lifetime to find happiness, and only a moment for everything you've ever known that really meant something to vanish. I don't know how you feel about it, but it just doesn't seem to be fair that we're living only to die."

I was speechless and lost for words when he hugged me and told me, "Brother, never let me go." Then he left. I stood there at the door, paralyzed with apprehension and clueless about what to do.

My family arrived home an hour later with pampered smiles, and I sat on the couch unresponsive as they attempted to get my attention to show me their prettifying transformation. Cat asked me what was wrong, but I wasn't able to say anything. She tried getting my attention again with a touch.

"Yeah?" I said.

"Are you okay?"

"I don't know."

Then the doorbell rang and Cat went to answer it.

Inside came Jalyn grinning before me, and said, "I went to visit my dad, but he told me to come and play with Aajani at your house and to give you something." She took her backpack off her tiny shoulders, reached inside, and pulled out an envelope with my name on it. Sensing a foreboding sensation, I told Jalyn to go play while I opened it up. Inside were instructions for me to procure his belongings, and the names of individuals he would like to bequest and allocate his personal effects to. His manifesto also contained contact numbers for his family and the passcode to his garage for entry.

I put the note down and asked Jalyn, "Who drove you over to visit your dad?"

"My mom. She and my dad needed to talk."

My phone rang while I was talking to her. I looked at my caller ID, and it was Jackie. I answered the phone and he asked me, "Did my daughter make it to your house?"

"Yeah," I said.

"Did she give you the envelope?"

"Yeah, she did. Is everything okay?"

"No," he said. "Make sure Jalyn don't come home. I love you."

I ran out the front door toward his home with my phone still up to my ear, because he didn't disconnect the call. I overheard a chilling scream from Lynda in the background saying, "Jackie, no!" Next, I heard him say to her, "It was all a dream!" Then one single gunshot echoed through the phone.

I dropped my cell phone when I heard the menacing sound, but I continued my advancement to his house until I saw his garage door open with Lynda lying on the concrete, motionless. Blood poured out onto the pavement from the gaping hole in her head.

Witnessing that macabre scene temporarily drained all the strength from my body, causing me to slow my stride to a complete stop, and then I took a knee and tried not to hyperventilate. It felt like someone had just pick-pocketed me out of my precious breath, because my breathing was very shallow as I began wheezing like an asthmatic sufferer. Just then, my lungs powered into overtime like an industrial generator to supply my muscles with the necessary oxygen they needed.

While I was still immobilized, Jackie came into view. He walked out of his garage as if he was oblivious to his surroundings, clutched Lynda by her legs, and dragged her body back inside the garage. As he stood up, he noticed me watching. All I could do was stare into his indecipherable, blank eyes before his garage door lowered to the ground.

Somehow, I recovered right away and sprinted as fast as I could to his garage. I reached inside my pocket, fumbling anxiously for the manifesto with the listed passcode to open his garage, until I remembered I had left the letter on the couch. Attempting to recall the code from memory, I quickly tried different series of four digits that I believed could be the entry code, but none of them worked. Then I heard a loud, ominous, single gunshot.

My body jolted to a halt and my heart stopped, because I knew the sound I heard was Jackie cashing out. I stood there, stoned for a while, until several police cars turned onto the street. The officers exited their vehicles armed and cautiously approached the property.

After I verified and authenticated the realism of my surroundings, I involuntarily began walking toward my home with a lethargic momentum in every step while all the sound around me was inaudible; melancholy had set into my quintessence, dispersing an infestation of confusion. Surreal would be close to an accurate portrayal of my state of mind. I continued my trancelike stroll in the direction of my house, mystified and unable to make sense of it all.

I incoherently walked back inside my home with a zombielike mannerism, detached, like I'd just received a frontal lobotomy from Dr. Victor Frankenstein. I entered our living room to see Cat holding the manifesto, looking disconcerted; she said, "Please don't tell me . . ."

The room was lukewarm, but I felt a coldness overcome me that only a donor cadaver who just had his heart ripped away from his chest would feel. Then the heaviest tear formed in my eye and silently fell like an anvil. "Where are the kids?"

She started to lightly tremble and then said, "They're all in the back room."

I paused for a moment and looked away for strength. Then I turned back to face her and said, "Jackie just executed Lynda, and then he killed himself. They're not here anymore."

She closed her eyes, clenched her fists, and then cried out, "No!"

Cat's sobbing was shrill, so I took her by the shoulders and led her into the bedroom so the kids wouldn't know. After securing Cat, I went into the back room and watched his daughter play with our children without a care in the world, just as innocent as a child should be. She looked up and noticed me watching her and said, "What?"

I shook my head. "Nothing," I told her.

CHAPTER 11
ABYSMAL

Over the next few weeks, I was still unable to pull it together, seemingly trapped in an indefinite state of psychological limbo. One late afternoon on my physical convalescence hiatus, I was sitting in my habitual lawn chair in the back yard, stargazing, when Cat appeared and asked if I would be eating dinner with the family. I informed her that I wasn't hungry.

She confronted me, saying, "Honey, I understand what you're going through, and that's why it was in our best interest not to go on vacation. But all you do is walk around the house and ignore us like you're the only one home. You still have a family here that needs you to be involved."

In my poignant ambience, I said, "I'm sorry, but I could've saved both of them. Now, because of me, their daughter is an orphan."

"Baby," Cat said gently, "you didn't have the professional training to prevent a situation to this degree; you did all you could do, and he knew that you were a very good friend. Yes, Jalyn doesn't have either of her parents any longer. But, she's not living in an orphanage, or with strangers . . . she's with Lynda's family now. They have a beautiful heart, so we know that they're going to love her just as much as her parents did."

"Well, I still feel responsible."

"You shouldn't. Also, you've been suffering from sleep deprivation for quite some time now, which could be contributing to your guilt. Maybe you can see a doctor about prescribing you some sleeping pills, so you can start getting some adequate rest."

"My issue isn't going to sleep, it's staying asleep," I told her.

"So, you're having nightmares about what happened, right?"

My nightmares were unrelated to my friend's death, but I couldn't tell her what they were about, so I didn't say anything.

"So I see that you're still shutting me out." She turned to go back into the house and then hesitated with her hand on the doorknob, tilted her head over her shoulder, and said, "I'm pregnant!"

I was dispassionately stoned in my ambiguous disposition hearing Cat's official communiqué about something that sounded like a baby. Unresponsively, I stared at her without murmuring a word and watched her enter the house, visibly displeased over my silence. I spent the rest of the night outdoors, restless and discombobulated.

The next afternoon, while I was lying in bed watching television, Cat entered and told me that we have to talk about the conceptional matter we had at hand.

I said, "I don't understand how you got pregnant, because we haven't done anything in a while since my sexual prowess been on the fritz."

"Three weeks and two days since you touched me, to be exact," she said.

"Damn, I've been sugar-free for that long, huh?"

"Well, that's not unusual, considering what's going on with you right now."

"Hmm," I said. "So how long you been knowing?"

"Almost a week . . . I wanted to tell you sooner, but there has been this enormous detachment between us, and I didn't—"

"I understand, but I have given it some thought, and to be honest, I don't think this is a good time to have a child. As a matter of fact, I don't believe we should have any more children at all."

"So what are you implying?" said Cat.

"Well, don't make me spell it out; I think you can read between the lines."

She looked at me in disbelief, so I obliged her with my bluntness so my intentions weren't misconstrued. "T-E-R-M-I-N-A-T-E—terminate!"

"I can't believe you're suggesting that to me."

"I'm not suggesting—that's a directive."

"I'm going to excuse myself and allow you to marinate alone in that selfish, abominable directive, and maybe after you get some rest and come to your senses, we'll be able to talk with some civility." She left the room, shutting the door in a manner indicating her resentment.

A couple of days later, while I was reclining in the Hall of Valhalla watching Daytona Speedway racing for some interesting crashes, Cat came inside and stood over me with her arms folded. I took her silent posture as a sign of frustration, so I obliged her with the reluctant conversation I'd been avoiding.

"Our life is no adventurous nursery rhyme. You're not Mother Goose laying a golden egg and I'm not Johnny Appleseed fertilizing the little engines that could. If anything, I feel like Humpty Dumpty right now. The decisions we make are not going to be written down in some legendary fairytale, because the choices we make in the real world are attached to real-life consequences.

Listen, we can't afford any more kids, and besides, would you agree we have enough pretty, lovely babies?"

"It's not about having enough," she said, "it's about doing the right thing. Besides, don't you remember what you told me when we dined at that fancy restaurant?"

"Indulge me. What did I tell you?"

"You mentioned us having our own Blue Ivy . . . which is translation for a child in the context you used it."

Placing my beer down that now had the nerve to taste like insubordination. "Look, don't do that—you and I know that was only an expression of verbalized foreplay . . . which is translation for a figure of speech, not to be taken literally in the context I used it, all right!"

"You always think that you have a clever answer to everything . . . so tell me, professor, what you mean we can't afford another child when you have over sixty thousand dollars saved up?"

I avoided the question and said, "Every day, there are thousands of people around the world who terminate pregnancies for several reasons. It's their right and it's legal."

Gesturing quotation marks with her hands, she answered, "Well, I'm not going to be a part of that fraternity of quote-unquote *thousands*."

"Physically and emotionally, I only have enough for the family we already have," I told her. "I'm so overwhelmed right now with commitments and responsibilities that don't allow me the luxury to have any more to give. Even adoption isn't an option. I'm tapping out on this one and making an executive decision for us to terminate. I'm also going to look into scheduling myself an appointment to get a vasectomy so that we don't have this problem ever again."

"I'm not going to kill my child because you're having a difficult time right now, Michael; things will get better."

I thought for a moment about things getting better but finally said, "I don't think so."

"You're still greatly bothered about what happened to your friend," she said. "I am too. But life goes on and you need to live in the present, because security and happiness should be the most important things in our lives right now, not regret. You can't change what happened; you have a responsibility to us and we need you, so please, let's move on."

"I guess you're right . . . I just need a little more time."

"Okay, I'm going to give you more time to accept this pregnancy. I know you will make the right choice."

"I was referring to myself needing more time, not you," I said.

"What do you mean?" she asked.

"I don't want you to grow too attached to this pregnancy more than you already are, so your time is up. It's either now or never."

"I can't believe you're strong-arming me to murder!"

Standing up from my sedentary position, I asked her, "That's what you call it?"

"We will be taking away the opportunity for a human being, our very own child, to choose to live life just like me and you. Just because it's legal, that doesn't make it right at all," she shouted.

"I told you that I don't have any more of myself to give, and that goes for tomorrow and the next day and the next one," I shouted back.

"This is painful, and you shouldn't make promises you can't keep. Do you recall that day inside the therapist's office when you promised never to hurt me again? You crossed your heart and hoped to die!"

"Again," I said, "that was another figure of speech. Did you expect for me to sit crisscross apple sauce too? Don't be childish."

"No," Cat said, "I knew it was a metaphor, but I still assumed that you were sincere."

"Every now and then, things go awry—life can be funny like this sometimes. Why can't you be happy with what we already have? And like I told you, we can't afford another child because we're broke, goddamnit!"

She got closer and asked, "Why are we broke?"

"It's complicated," I said.

"I *did* graduate from college with a 3.96 GPA—try me."

We were nose-to-nose in a gridlock. I didn't want to inform her of the humiliating defeat I'd suffered from losing all our investment and savings, but I also didn't want to elude her any longer. I took a deep breath and sat in my chair so that the leather could embrace me, and finally said, "Cowboy ripped me off."

She shook her head and said, "What? But how?"

"He been running a Ponzi scheme on me the entire time I've known him. My money, our money, and everyone else's money entrusted to that degenerate prick is gone. It's a cold world."

"So, when did you find this out?" she said.

"The same night I came back home."

"I'm guessing then, those bite marks on your face and hands weren't from Miss Calico?"

"No," I said, "me and Cowboy fought and that was his yuck mouth chewing on me."

She gasped and said, "Oh my god! Well, you have to do something; don't let him get away with this. Call the police."

"Hey, let it go. I'm not getting the cops involved, so let's just forget about it."

"Forget about it? We're talking about fifty thousand dollars here, Michael!"

"No," I said, "try sixty-two thousand. I also gave him an additional twelve thousand of what I had in my savings and checking account too."

"Wow!" Cat held up her hand, pointed at her ring finger, and said, "so, how did you purchase this?"

"Credit." I said.

"Well, if you're not going to do something about this, I will. I'm calling the police."

Swiftly, she turned around and started walking into the house. Before she made it to the door, I jumped up and shouted, "No, you can't do that!"

She stopped, turned around, and said forcefully, "Why?"

Equally aggressively, I said, "Because he said he will kill you and our children! I'm a liability and a threat to his entire operation and that megalomaniac will do anything to protect his enterprise. Cat, just let it go, please!"

"Is that why you've been acting extra cautious and carrying your gun around everywhere?"

I nodded my head to confirm her evaluation. She then placed her hands over her face and said, "I've never felt so un-centered in my life, and I don't feel safe here anymore." She walked over to me and took off her ring and said, "I guess *Fairytopia* don't always last forever—you're going to need this more than me, because I'm going to have this baby. You were right when you said this is the real world. So this is the consequence. I pray that all the king's horses and all the king's men are able to put you back together again, Humpty Dumpty!" She handed me the engagement ring and walked out.

⇌⇋

Within the next couple of days, she and the kids packed their belongings and literally moved out, to my disbelief. My quality of life at that point was withering; angst was intensifying rapidly at a fast deteriorating rate without any sign of an intermission. Hitting rock bottom would've been an understatement to describe my circumstances. If the bottom had a bottom; I was too deep and disoriented to realize which way was up. The only attachment I had to hope felt like a crusty dingle berry entangled in the crevice of a hyena's anus on a hot safari day in the Serengeti bush. Such a shame that the closest semblance I could compare myself to was a piece of shit trapped in the crack of a scavenger's ass. Misery seemed to stage a ubiquitous permanency that was inescapable, as well as spurring the worse uninterrupted wretchedness I've ever felt and causing an ocean of saddening hopelessness.

After a few weeks of avoiding phone calls and random visitors knocking at my door, my mother showed up and insisted that I let her in. I stood resolute, like a sentry on the inside of my locked door, and I said, "Not today, Ma . . . maybe tomorrow, okay?"

"You said that yesterday," she said.

"Well, tomorrow you might get lucky."

She started kicking the bottom half of the door and said, "If you don't let me in today, I'm going to call the sheriff."

"Who, Matt Dillon?"

"What?" she asked.

"Today must be Sunday," I suggested.

"What are you trying to say?"

I explained my theory on how I was able to guess which day of the week it was, saying, "Because I know on Sunday mornings, you watch old reruns of *Gunsmoke*. You're showing your age right now, people don't say that they're calling the sheriff anymore, now they say that they're calling the police." After I embarrass her, she made it very clear that if I didn't answer the door instantly, she was going to call the police department to come and check on me. With the threat of her contacting law enforcement, I reluctantly allowed her to come into my squalor. When she came inside she said, "Son, you look like an alley cat . . . I hope you're not in here licking yourself like one. When was the last time you bathed?"

"Ma, I'm a grown man . . . I don't bathe, I take showers."

"Well, it doesn't look like you have been doing that either." I didn't respond because I didn't want to validate her statement with the truth. "Judging from your appearance, it's no secret that hygiene isn't close to being a priority in your life." Then she pointed her finger in my face and said, "I hope you haven't been in here scratching and sniffing yourself—I raised you better than that."

I twitched my face and then I lied a little when I said, "I don't be doing that . . . besides, I thought your Bible teaches that only God can judge?"

"Well," she said, "I'm going to have to pray for forgiveness twice today, because I'm going to tell you again. Judging from your appearance, it's no secret—"

"Ma, you can't be coming up in here strong-arming me. I'm bigger than you."

She then tugged at my shirt and said, "You aren't as big as you used to be, so I know that you haven't been eating . . . your clothes look like they're hang gliding off your body because you're so frail."

I said, "Oh, yeah, I didn't tell you . . . I'm on an emergency diet to get down to a size one, because I saw this nice bikini on the QVC channel that I would like to fit into by the summer."

"Boy, don't get uppity with me!"

"I apologize; I'm a little tired right now. My appetite hasn't been in the mood for any nourishment. Besides, food is overrated anyway; less is best."

She turned from me to study my interior remodeling project and then pinched her nose. "What in the hell is that smell? If this is the best of what you've been doing with the less of your time, I'm not impressed. This cesspool really worries me, son, because it looks like a citywide dumping ground in here. I've never seen so many flies in one house. You should be on *Hoarders* for this crap!"

With that assessment, she began her trek through my homemade landfill. After taking a few steps, she said, "I'm afraid to go any further because I don't know where you be using the bathroom at—I should've brung a HAZMAT suit."

"Come on, Ma, I'm not a beast, and just like you said, you raised me better than that. Even if I didn't use the toilet, I would've at least buried my excrement."

She then whispered underneath her breath as though I couldn't hear her. "Your feces *could* be buried beneath all this garbage."

She stumbled through my repugnant home with indiscriminate litter everywhere that made my confines indistinguishable from the debris left after the Battle of the Little Bighorn—the only thing missing being a twelve-hundred-pound Civil War field artillery cannon.

After she unappreciatively surveyed my collage of disorganized artwork, she looked at me and asked, "When was the last time you slept?"

"I don't know," I said.

She stepped closer to me and said, "I figured you'd say something like that, and that's why I bought you this." She opened up a bag and pulled out a weird-looking apparatus and said, "Here, hang this above your bed."

"What is this?" I asked.

"It's a dreamcatcher. I found it in the Goodwill store. The American Indian people have used this for centuries to help block bad dreams and catch good ones. Try it."

I wasn't optimistic about its effectiveness, but I desperately needed some good sleep, so I was willing to give it a chance. I grabbed a sticky hook out of my toolbox and hung the device on the wall above my bed.

My mother came to my bedroom door and said, "I'm going to straighten up your home and try to kill some of these flies while you're getting some rest, okay?"

I acquiesced and then laid diagonally across my bed, not bothering to get beneath the sheets because I knew sleep was not promised. I began to get a little drowsy, so I whispered to Mr. Sandman to give me something pleasant. But yet again, he was a dream-crusher, serving me cruelty with his draconian humor; another one of my many ominous dreams of Cowboy dressed in black garb with a hood, looking like the grim reaper holding a scythe in the shadows, brutalizing my family and me.

We were all trapped inside a dank, poorly lit dungeon that he'd named "The House of Discipline" with a gallery of intimidating medieval torturing devices to atone us. My family was grouped together, terror-stricken, hugging, and crying. They also looked emaciated from starvation, with shackles around their ankles connected to chains that bound them to metal rings fixed into the concrete foundation. To intensify their fear, three bloodthirsty Rottweilers, each wearing a spiked collar around its neck, encircled them, brandishing a flesh-eating set of serrated teeth, barking ferociously. Helplessly, I was separated from them, being hoisted above the ground locked inside a huge birdcage with the fattest *Oompa Loompa* dressed only in a diaper harassing me.

My short-statured antagonizer wore a fuchsia-colored wig with two braided pigtails that hung on both sides of his head; along with the most obvious fake freckles. He skipped around the outside of my enclosure, smearing on GloZellGreen lipstick galore and humming an irritating, children's nursery rhyme, occasionally stopping to poke me with a sharp stick. Shrewdly, I was able to pick the lock secretively with a small, fragmented splint of wood that I pulled from one of my many stab wounds. After freeing myself from the suspended coop, I leapt out with a flying Superman punch and knocked the midget semi-unconscious. Then bizarrely, I realized that the Oompa Loompa had the face of Donald J. Trump while he curled in the fetal position, sucking his thumb. I picked up the spear that had been used to perforate my torso and used it as a lethal weapon to slay the savage dogs.

After our tormentors had been eliminated, I approached my family to release them. But before I could rescue them, Cowboy appeared out of nowhere and brutally slaughtered them with his swinging blade in one fatal swipe.

I jolted out of my wretched nightmare, waking up in a cold sweat. I snatched the whatchamacallit off the wall and ripped it up, because there was nothing righteous about that contraption.

I came irritably out of my bedroom into an organized, pleasant home. My mother was sitting on the couch and asked me if I slept okay.

"Hell, no, life sucks, but who gives a damn."

She stood up, walked over to me and gently touched my face with both hands. "Son, I care. And so does God."

I took her hands off my face and said, "Oh my goodness, don't start that."

She took me by my hand, led me to the dinette table, and asked me to sit down with her. I half-heartedly appeased her. However, while I was awaiting some type of lengthy oration for guidance that I most likely would ignore, she got out of her chair, looking boggled, and began searching underneath the table and around it.

"What you looking for?" I asked.

She sat back down and started tapping her finger on the tabletop. "Hmm, I got some anointed blessing oil from my church and placed it right here on your table, but now it's not here. I had plans on using it to cleanse your home once you'd awoken."

I rubbed my eyes to adjust my vision from the blare of waking up. "Well, things don't grow legs and walk away, Ma. I'm sure there's a logical explanation why it's not where you put it."

"Like what?"

"Like leaving your miracle juice at home on your own table . . . you didn't bring it, all right?"

With assurance, she said, "But I know for a fact that I placed it here."

"Well, with your age, facts are not dependable," I said.

"Okay, but if it comes up, just let me know so I can—"

"Listen, even if the U.S. Coast Guard found your blessed holy oil, it wouldn't work. It's totally useless, right along with the tribal feathers and your prayers. If I was gullible and generous enough to lead you on to think that I believe in that spiritual nonsense, you'd probably bring some two thousand-year-old sacred monkey bones in here next to cleanse out whatever you and your holy-rolling syndicate are trying to get rid of. Thank you, Mother, but I'm fine."

She fidgeted around before she said, "Michael, come to church with me today."

I jumped up out of my chair. "No! You know I don't do religion!"

"You have to believe that when prayers go up, blessings come down. Please pray with me."

Sharply, I retorted, "It doesn't work, especially for those humbling themselves until hell freezes over waiting on a prayer. If there are any sign of blessings raining down . . . it's all too obvious to me that those blessings are exclusively aimed at the *haves*, who could care less if there's a God or not, and unavailable for the *have nots*. It shouldn't take much for a God who's all-knowing and omnipotent to show some technical skills and place a GPS tracker on those prayer orders he's receiving from the faithful. Punctuality and accuracy should be his mission statement answering prayers, to validate that there is some reliability in this faith of yours. I don't think that I'm being presumptuous when I say that there's a lack of professionalism going on with this corporation in the sky. Regular folks on this planet rock will lose their jobs and find themselves in the unemployment line for incompetencies like this. So, just in case you're a little disoriented right now, I need to let you know that I'm not a wide-eyed, naive little child no more."

"In your current condition, will it hurt if you call upon him for help?" she said.

"I'm not doing it."

"You have everything to gain if he answers your prayers, and nothing to lose if he doesn't. Please just do it for me."

"Ma, you're being too pushy right now, and it's irritating me. I'm sorry, Mother, but I just can't do it."

"Why?" she asked.

Fervent with agitation, I aggressively said, "All that praying we done to improve our conditions while I was growing up—God never did anything for us that we couldn't do for ourselves. The times I personally prayed to stop all those beatings I took from your ex-husband who had the audacity to call himself my father never stopped. Where was your God when a child needed him, huh? Yeah, I'm talking about your high school sweetheart who swept you right off your feet. What a guy. You know that motherfucker despised me; I saw the hate in his eyes every day when he had to look at me. I could hear the disgust roll from his tongue when he had to speak to me, and he charged his anger to my flesh with all those beatings I received with his big black belt. I had to pay his inflated cost for myself existing with painful welts covering my entire body and saturated in blood, sweat, and tears. All those years he depersonalized me by addressing me as *boy*, and he didn't give me the courtesy or respect to call me by the namesake that he passed to me until I was fifteen years old. There was one time when I was a kid, I can recall asking him to watch *Excalibur* with me—I loved that movie . . . it finally felt like we was bounding like father and son, and I smiled the whole time."

"But I'll never forget what he said when the movie ended. It broke my heart when he stood up and looked at me and said, 'Hmm, that looks like a film for dreamers,' and then he walked out. He and I have never had anything meaningful. The only things we shared in common was distance and silence. If I never see that tyrant again, it would be too soon; even if I bump into someone who looks like him, I'm going to give him a silent lullaby with some Nyquil he can't drink. I'm going to hurt him bad. Do you understand what it's like to be a child waking up from a nightmare to face a monster more terrifying than the ghoul of your dreams every single day? There was no one to protect us from the man that was supposed to be doing the protecting. I prayed, and I prayed, and I prayed for it to stop, but my prayers fell on deaf ears because your God abandoned me. Now I understand why Jesus wept. So, if he didn't do anything visible for me as a desperate, fragile child, why would he do something now as an adult?"

My mom broke down into tears and said, "Michael, I'm sorry I didn't do enough to stop the abuse. I'm so sorry."

I hugged her and said, "Ma, it's not your fault, you were a victim too. Don't blame yourself because of that dirt bag."

"I could have done something," she said. "I may not have been able to stop him physically, but I could've left him. I wasn't strong. I'm sorry for failing you, Michael. I'm so sorry, son."

I held her tighter. "It's okay, Ma, you have always been great to me. We have always had something very special, and that's why I love you so much." I pulled her away and made a gesture with my hands to bring attention to my silhouette and said, "Look at me—I made it through all right. I'm just a little screwed up on the inside, but you can't see my insecurities with the naked eye. Just look at the bright side of things: the hardship I went through made me a better father to my own children than he ever was to me. Besides, I made a covenant with myself a long time ago. I told myself when I grow up and have my own family, I would cherish them like there was no tomorrow and never strike them because I wanted my family to love me genuinely without fear in their heart, and I've accomplished that."

She looked at me and said, "You sure have, son, and I'm proud of you for overcoming that . . . may each one teach one."

"That's a noble slogan," I said, "but how about each one protects one as well. You know, that would be a generous campaign to assure all individuals a trusted physical guardian angel as a safeguard against abuse like that. The benefit of a child being raised in a safe environment and provided with a good role model until adulthood is priceless. Just imagine how many lives would be saved, or how many valuable relationships would remain intact, preventing people from losing hearts with their loved ones? This would be a worthy slogan that doesn't discriminate, and could generate unimaginable results, setting precedence. Hmm, imagine a world like that, where everyone wins."

"I like that," she said. "I believe you would've been a fine politician or community organizer . . . give me another hug."

After a moment of our locked sentimental embrace, I tried to pull away but couldn't because she was standing on my bare feet with her heels penetrating through my epidermis like a Texas-size diamond-tip oil drill bit.

Nicely, I said, "Ma, I really don't want to spoil this moment, but you're hurting my toes with those secondhand Easter Sunday church shoes you're wearing."

She got off my foot before causing any real damage and playfully hit me. "Boy, do you know how much I paid for these down at the Goodwill store?"

"What, a dollar?"

"No, they had a stain on them, so I talked them down to fifty cents." We laughed, and after our short merriment she gave me a serious look and said, "Michael, you know I'm not going to give up, so what would it take?"

"Oh my goodness, not this again." I thought about it, and I decided to tell her something creative to keep her off my back about her God forever. "I'll tell you what it'll take, okay?"

I could tell that I had her undivided attention when she asked me to allow her to sit down first.

With a studious look, she said, "Okay, tell me."

"If your God could present himself and give me an immortal to mortal interface, so I can ask him a few questions . . . I'll be a believer."

"Son, I'm sorry to tell you, but it doesn't work like that. You just have to have faith."

"You're asking me to have faith in something I can't see?"

"You can't see the wind either, but you know it's there." she said.

"It's not the same, so let's end this conversation because I can see that you would use anything to endorse your magical *sky daddy*."

She got up from her seat and said, "*You* are a mess. I'm going to let God deal with you on his terms, but in the meantime, can you see if you could get some professional therapy? At least do that for me, Michael."

"I'll think about it," I said.

"I don't know why you have to be so stubborn, or what I'm going to do with you. Let me get out of here before you rub off on me. God knows there is not enough room in this world for two of you."

I chuckled as a sign of approval of her truest statement thus far. Then I placed my hands on her shoulders and pointed her body toward the door to remind her about her exit. She wasn't too thrilled with the signal because she shrugged off my hands and pointed her finger in my face. "Boy, don't rush me! Since you rushing, how about you rush and crack a window to get this odorous stench out your house? You better not allow this nice home to become a pigsty again . . . and get this chandelier fixed so it can put some light in your life."

"I'm sorry," I said. "Is there anything else, your majesty?"

"Don't patronize me with that type of attitude."

I conceded her complaint to extradite her departure and apologized. We both walked to the front door, and I held it open because I knew she wasn't done gabbing until she was comfortably inside her vehicle. A few feet before she reached her car, she turned around and delivered her final maternal advice. "At least get out of that house before you go stir-crazy." I simply formulated the smile of a respectful lad and waved good-bye.

After some time, my home fell back into noticeable disrepair. My physical appearance along with my psychological well-being was beginning to show signs of corrosion, like a rusty pipe underneath a dilapidated home in the slums. I was inundated with grief over everything I've been through up to this point, and I felt like regurgitated ghetto vomit mixed with sorrow in a crock-pot waiting to be consumed again. It became more and more difficult to laugh or even smile at things I used to enjoy. Television was my only outlet and companion, and I lived a vicarious, medieval life on my sofa as I watched episode after episode of *Game of Thrones*.

Late one Saturday, while I was channel-surfing other programs to watch on television, I came across an infomercial that encouraged people to endorse a healthy vitality in the strength of language by promoting how positive motivational words could manifest themselves into your aura and make a significant improvement in a person's life. The commentator was an inspiring older gentleman in his seventies who had the athleticism to become a triathlete. He accredited his youthful inspiration to the late James Dean mantra, "Dream as if you'll live forever—live as if you'll die today."

Like a switch, I had a light-bulb moment that revitalized my optimism. I jumped up off the couch and said, "Now that's what I need to do—I need to start living again." I got spirited into going out and having a great time. I turned on some stimulating, upbeat-tempo music before dashing into the restroom to shave the scraggly mane off my face. It looked like a conglomerate of swarming Africanized honeybees trying to pollinate my jawbone. After seeing my leather for the first time in eons, I gave myself an open-handed smack as a gesture of endearment and then jumped into the shower to sanitize and exfoliate the accessories. I put on some fresh clothes and primped in the mirror for a minute or two before I asked who was the fairest of them all, but it wasn't much of a magical mirror to grant me a response. So I self-confirmed the reply myself by winking at the debonair, well-groomed gentleman that reflected back at me and excused myself like a distinguished count. Yours truly opened up the front door and high-stepped out of my home like a prized thoroughbred and said, "Hello, world!"

I got to the club and noticed it was full to capacity, and the wait to enter was at a standstill. I knew the bouncer, so he allowed me VIP entrance, bypassing all the people waiting in line. I got inside and received a generous reception from familiar faces as though I'd just been released from Alcatraz on a bum rap. Feeling like a local celebrity, I moseyed over to the bar and ordered myself a drink, to do as they do in Rome. After slamming down a double shot of Rémy Martin VSOP, I started fist pumping in the air like I was an intoxicated Guido on MTV's *Jersey Shore* reality show. The spacious club was jam-packed with zestful *party-a-holics*, and I was looking forward to having an awesome night.

I then glanced over my right flank to look at the elevated VIP section and saw my arch-nemesis Cowboy with his eyes already fixed on me. The undesirable megalomaniac cracked a pretentious smile, revealing a new set of teeth, which appeared to be replaced with platinum and diamonds, reflecting like a disco ball. He pointed his hand at me, simulating a gun, and blew his finger as he had routinely done in his mirror. While he antagonized me with an ostentatious grin, my facial expression was stone cold, articulating a grimacing gaze.

I fiercely made an identifiable effort to penetrate his beady eyes with the message of transparent animosity. That was the first time I ever wished I had Superman powers to zap someone into smithereens by way of using my deadly laser vision, until the bartender interrupted my phantasm and asked me if I would like another drink. After rejecting the second serving of cognac, I noticed that Cowboy was in company of a new entourage. They were some well-dressed hooligans with long, braided cornrows looking like Bone Thugs-n-Disharmony wearing sunglasses, fraternizing with some exotic-looking bimbos dressed like sluts. I left my post and walked around the club exasperated, until I decided that I couldn't tolerate being in the same space with Cowboy.

I walked toward the entrance to leave, but I was approached by a bartender extending a bottle of Patron to me. I told her that I didn't order the tequila, and she said that it was courtesy of Mr. Cowboy. The bottle had a small gift card attached to a miniature chain around the collar of the glass. I opened it up, and it read, "*Bang! Bang!*" I looked over at him; he and his goons had their drinking glasses in the air for a toast. I grabbed the bottle from the waitress, popped the cork, held the bottle upside down, and began pouring its contents onto the floor.

While it continued to spill, I told her, "Make sure you tell him that I don't scare easy, and the next time we meet, I'm going to take his new smile and drill it up his shitty ass so he can get a flavor of how blood diamonds really taste." I gave the waitress the bottle back and left the club, infuriated.

I was driving down the highway, heading home, when someone pulled up behind me with the bright lights on. Showing roadway etiquette, I steered into the other lane so that the motorist could pass, but the driver switched lanes as well. I slowed my vehicle down below the speed limit thinking that the person would pass, but the vehicle slowed down with me too. Annoyed, I reached inside my armrest and grabbed my gun, and that's when I heard a gunshot that put a hole through my rear window.

My heart started pounding with the force of a sledgehammer as I fumbled with my weapon like Fredo Corleone in *The Godfather*.

It landed on the other side of the vehicle on the passenger floor. I pressed down on the gas pedal as hard as I could with my foot to accelerate speed, but with its size, my H2 Hummer seemed to move like a wounded tyrannosaur. Quickly, I grabbed an umbrella from the pouch of the seat and attempted to use the handle to retrieve my weapon, but wasn't able to. The other vehicle was still behind me flashing the high beams, making it difficult for me to identify who it was.

I had about another mile to go until the next exit, when the vehicle tried to get beside me. Defensively, I swerved into the other lane to thwart the advancement and continued to do so every time the driver attempted to get beside me. During one of the attempts, I miscalculated my maneuver, and the driver was able to gain access next to me. That's when I noticed the vehicle was a white Range Rover. The windows were darkly tinted so I couldn't see who was inside, even as we rode side by side.

At that moment, the rear passenger window rolled down just enough for a hand holding a firearm to appear. "Oh shit, it just got real!" I yelled.

I ducked my head at the same time a double shot shattered my driver's and passenger window. While hunching over, I slammed on the brakes, making the tires squeal. Then peeked over the dashboard while my vehicle was slowing down and noticed that the armed bandits had Florida license plates. The Range Rover kept going so I accelerated and hastily veered onto the shoulder of the road, and got off the interstate at the next exit, shaking like a scaredy-cat.

Traveling home, I listened to the gust of wind whistling through my bullet-riddled H2 Hummer like the thematic tune to *The Good, the Bad and the Ugly*. But Clint Eastwood would have never dropped his weapon in a duel, so I was disappointed that my *True Grit* moment for a showdown was molested by an inappropriate set of butterfingers. Worst of all, I couldn't believe that I'd taken advice from an infomercial commentated by a geriatric guy with a bucket list, encouraging people to be audacious daredevils. His quote was more fitting for adrenaline junkies who engage in hazardous activities, like a parachutist who gets a rush from skydiving and freefalling from airplanes, or a zoophilic deep-sea scuba diver who has a fixation with sharks. But certainly not for the average faint-hearted person who wants to live a prolonged centenarian life like myself. I should've obeyed my first instincts to remain in the safety of my home and create new tricks on my professional-grade yo-yo. My summarizing intuition utterly failed me, because it didn't see the bigger picture. Consequently, that remiss allowed me to be influenced by a figurative quotation that was manufactured by a celebrity who popularized being rebellious. James Dean's name is synonymous with his classic movie *Rebel Without a Cause*, and ironically encountered a premature death involving a reckless car crash, dying at the early age of twenty-four. Living fast and dying young will forever be his signature, which catapulted his posthumous stardom into the stratosphere of earthly demigods, along with a few other young, iconic figures that has captivated many people with their impactful temporal presence. I didn't want to initiate an early death certificate by living on the edge like an Aerosmith song, or challenge the threat of going against the odds with risky activities. Having a typical family is adventurous enough; that comes in a variety of packages, guaranteeing a limitless quantity of nonfatal adrenaline rushes and thrills to last a lifetime.

    I pulled up in front of my home with suspicion, and cautiously entered my domicile with my handgun in tow. Before I relaxed, I checked and cleared every room because I wasn't sure if I was safe. After ensuring no one was lying in wait inside my home, I paced my carpet, trying to figure out if that incident was a random mistake of identity, or if it was a deliberate assassination attempt on my life. I connected the dots and determined that it was Cowboy and his cronies without a doubt, because prior to that, I had a nonphysical altercation with that psychopath inside the club. It was unquestionably a cold, premeditated, calculating hit. I believed another attack was imminent at my dwelling, and began to take every precaution to preserve my life. I went into Rambo survivalist mode in three point two seconds to protect myself and to turn the structural design of my home into a military standard-issued battlefield-defensive encampment.

Entering my armory, I put on my ammo vest, which was loaded with an assortment of magazines, and then pulled out several weapons and strategically placed them around my home as a contingency safeguarding strategy. I wanted to have the advantage of dominating the firepower anywhere to suppress their attack and terminate the targets on-site. In the event of close hand combat, I strapped my hip holster to my waist that held a Native American Indian tomahawk so I could scalp my enemy like a bald eagle. I even considered drilling a six-inch-diameter hole through the roof, so that I could wedge a protruding periscope through it. That renovation was guaranteed to give me a panoramic view of the outside landscape for early proximity detection on any hostile approaching enemies. But I scratched that idea because the homeowners' association may not have agreed with that remodeling project. Compensating for that, I improvised a complex system of early detection from within, using domestic supplies.

I got creative with an assortment of simplistic household items, starting with basic duct tape, and raided my children's arts and crafts container for their knitting yarn and bells. When I was finished, I had designed a low-grade, sophisticated alert monitoring system that was just as effective as any high-tech burglar alarm on the market. Then I pulled out my all-terrain military-grade sleeping bag and tactfully set up a command center in the middle of my living room. I had more than enough ammunition, plus a sufficient amount of food to last me for weeks, along with an unlimited supply of municipal tap water. Furthermore, I was well stocked with provisions and logistically prepared for guerilla warfare, and my self-discipline had enough stamina to defend my fort indefinitely.

When I was done, I stood in my living quarters and marveled over my impressive stronghold. *It would take a conqueror with the might of Genghis Khan to defeat me*, I thought. Now confident that I was prepared for apocalyptica, all I had to do at that point was wait patiently for the perpetrators to fall into my ambush and get perforated with full metal jackets.

CHAPTER 12
PENITENCE

After a couple weeks of inactive dog days and lethargic nights in my foxhole, I began to get worn down by attrition from an inadequate rest regiment. Sleep was already a precious natural resource that I took for granted, but now it was an enemy to my endurance. While looking like *The Curious Case of Benjamin Button*, I had a critical decision to make. I could get enough rest so that I could effectively guard my post with some competency, which would also be counterproductive and compromise my safety by placing me in an unconscious vulnerable position. Or I could continue ingesting over-the-counter jet-alert pills in order to stay vigilant, and concurrently watch my health methodically fade into deterioration like an ailing senior citizen on a fast-track of poor health. Faced with these complicated obstacles, I began to elucidate the pros and cons for the best possible solution. In the midst of my syllogistic reasoning, there was a knock on the door.

I was startled at first and then tactfully approached the access point with my twelve-gauge shotgun and carefully peered through the peephole. It appeared to be a group of nonaggressive civilians soliciting some sort of random product. I placed my back up against the door and said, "I don't need whatever you have; go away." That's when I heard someone say, "Daddy?"

Confused, I rubbed my eyes and turned around to glance through the peephole again. This time with a clearer vision, I saw my daughters appearing before me like Little Bo Peeps. It'd been so long since I'd seen or had any loving interaction with my family, or with any sentient being for that matter, but I didn't want them to see me like I was and said, "Oh, I'm sorry girlies, I thought y'all was somebody else . . . but umm, this is really not a good time to visit, okay?"

I heard a synchronized chorus coming from all three of them, saying, "Daddy, please." It was the sweetest, dovelike vocal, conveying a convincing language that affectionately told me they missed me greatly.

I didn't want to disappoint them, so I placed my weapon inside the front guest closet and opened the door. They were all too happy to see me and propelled their little bodies at me with a firm sentimental hug that should have exhumed a mutual feeling from me, but something was wrong. I didn't feel the same.

My daughters came inside, noticed my camouflage apparel, and observed my military staging area in the interior of the home. My oldest daughter Aajani pivoted three hundred and sixty degrees with her arms flared in the air and said, "What the what?"

I was perplexed about her ungrammatical structure of the English language and said, "Huh?"

She addressed me with an animated attitude with her hands on her hips, simulating her mother's mannerism, and said, "It smells like gunpowder in here, and your house looks *ratchet*. Are you having a midlife crisis?"

"No!" I said.

"Well, what you been doing?" she asked.

I told her that I was bored and decided to get some exercise by doing some combat training, and ordered all of them not to touch anything. She was doubtful and inquisitive about my spontaneous explanation and said, "Really, Dad? Did you have to build a fort in the living room and wear that camouflage uniform like you're in the jungle? Why couldn't you just play your *Call of Duty* video game?"

I wasn't prepared for the questioning, so I said, "Look, you're asking too many questions—y'all thirsty?"

She said, "Well, Mama said that you're paranoid because you've gone crazy."

"Your mother told you that?"

"Daddy have you gone cray-cray?" she asked.

"No," I told her, "your mama was only joking. How about y'all go into Valhalla and watch television, and let me put this stuff up so that we all can get comfortable."

She said, "Okie dokie, but can we have something to eat first?"

"I don't have anything to eat right now, but how about if I order you girls a triple pepperoni from Pizza Hut and have it delivered?" They were delighted to hear that, and willfully consented to my request to enter my lair. While they were secure inside and unmindful of all the munitions I had scattered around, I went to work retrieving everything that could endanger them. I broke down my command center and disengaged my homemade monitoring system along with relocating my cache of weapons underneath my bed inside the master bedroom. Then I changed my tactical uniform into something more appropriate.

Not long after completing the task of kid-proofing my home to a safer environment, the pizza deliverer showed up with everyone's favorite. I went inside my man-quarters to announce to them that our hot chow had just arrived, and that's when I noticed that my NASCAR limited-edition sports memorabilia table lamp was lying on the floor broken.

I instantly got upset. "Who did this?"

My two oldest girls pointed and spoke at the same time. "It was Bamm-Bamm!"

While eyeballing the knee-high destroyer, I cocked my head to one side and said, "Haven't I told you to keep those little destructive hands off my stuff?"

She looked nervous, but then Aajani spook up and said, "I'm sorry, but it was mostly my fault because I was trying to teach her how to twerk upside down with a handstand on your couch, but she lost her balance and fell over on your lamp and knocked it down."

"I can't even replace that lamp. What have I told you about dirty dancing? What are you trying to do . . . grow up to be a world-class stripper? There isn't a Fortune 500 human resource department in the world that's going to be looking for that on your resume. This is your final caveat. If I catch or hear about one of you—"

Aajani held up her hand and said, "Excuse me, Daddy, but what is a *caveat*?"

"Put your damn hands down—you're not in school. That means a warning. So, again, if I catch or hear about any one of you popping your butt again, you going to be breaking big rocks to little rocks like little convicts in Alcatraz until you're eighteen years old. You got that? Now get out of here, and go wash your hands so y'all can eat."

They shamefully held their heads down and marched out of my man cave in a single-file line with Bamm-Bamm in the rear, saying, "I'm sorry, Daddy." I didn't respond because I was too crushed about losing that precious lamp. I really loved that lamp. Aaniyah then yelled in the distance, "Dad, we're going to catch cooties because your house is still a mess."

While we were at the dinner table eating, the girls got antsy and started frolicking around with each other like they were exuberant toy soldiers on the Nickelodeon channel. Then, unsurprisingly, Aaniyah accidentally knocked over Bamm-Bamm's grape soda, causing it to spill all over the table and drip on the carpet. After cleaning up the annoying spill, I sat down on the couch and operated the television to get myself updated with the latest current events while the kids finished eating. It was very frustrating for me to listen to the news while the kids were out of control, throwing pepperoni like Frisbees at each other across the table. I was too exhausted to reprimand them, so I pretended it wasn't happening until one struck me in the face and stuck to the side of my cheek. That irritated me a lot, but I mentally counted to ten and kept my cool before I stood up and said, "Y'all doing a little too much, so I'm going to the bedroom to get some rest."

Aajani skipped up to me and said, "Daddy, let's play Daddy's Angels."

"What's that?" I said.

"It's a fun game where we get to be three street-wise detectives who get cases to solve from their mysterious boss, and we have to use walkie-talkies."

"That sounds like a '70s television series called *Charlie's Angels*."

"What's that, Daddy?"

"A TV show that sounds similar to the game you want to play."

"I've never seen it," she said. "I just learned this game from my new friend who lives next door to mom's house. Please, Dad, can we play? It's really fun."

"Maybe next time, sweetheart," I told her.

"Come on, Dad, don't be a buzz kill. We want to have fun; you don't play with us anymore like you used to."

"I'm sorry . . . y'all go ahead and play it without me. I promise I'll make it up to you somehow. Just give me a break for now."

She was disappointed to hear me default on my extracurricular duties as a father again, so she hunched her shoulders and whined back to the dinner table with a slow-moving stroll. Pretending to be unfazed by her dramatics, I entered my bedroom and straddled my bed, thinking, *oh my goodness, I used to dote on them with all the tolerance in the world, but now everything they do seems to be so goddamn annoying. Fuck, I need a sabbatical from the entire planet. I can't do it— I'm just not cut out for being a father right now.*

After coaching myself to keep it together, my time alone inside the bedroom felt sacred, until Bamm-Bamm burst into the room and destroyed my tranquility with some obnoxious child's play. I was agitated with her lack of respect for my safe haven and told her firmly to get out. With an apologetic expression on her face, she retraced her footsteps the same way she came in, and closed the door. I got up and locked it, then within ten minutes, Aaniyah knocked on the door and told me that Aajani had flooded the toilet.

"I'll take care of it when I come out," I blurted.

"Okay, so when are you coming out?"

"I don't know. Now go away." I then rolled over into a supine position, grabbed a pillow, and placed it over my head to drown out the loathsome noise. Within another five minutes, Aaniyah came banging on the door again, crying and screaming this time.

I terminated my siesta and sprung off the bed, flung the door open, and said, "What the hell is going on?"

Holding her face, she said, "Aajani slapped me."

With displeasure, I breached the confines of the room to address Aajani. "Did you slap her?"

She looked at me with contempt and shrugged her shoulders as though indicating that she was apathetic about her sister's accusation. I asked her again with more assertiveness. "Well, did you?"

Being evasive, she said, "I don't know."

Aaniyah spoke up and said, "She hit me hard on purpose, Dad, just because I accidently fell against her while we were playing, and I didn't mean to."

Aajani placed a hand on her hip, looked at Aaniyah, rolled her eyes and said, "Well, maybe I accidentally hit you back, so opsie-daisy."

With her confession, I decisively looked at Aajani and said, "What did I tell you about hitting? There's too many bullies out there for y'all to be fighting each other."

Nonchalantly, she shrugged her shoulders again and gave me an offensive expression. I went from annoyed to angry in one point two seconds, turned to Aaniyah, and said, "Hit her back!"

She tapered her sniveling and looked at me, confused. "Huh?"

"You heard me. Slap her back, just like she slapped you."

"I don't want to," Aaniyah said.

"You're going to do it. You don't let someone hit you and get away with it."

"But, Dad, I don't want to."

I got furious and got in Aaniyah's face, grabbed her by her shoulders, faced her toward Aajani, and pointed my finger at her bigger opponent and yelled, "Do it! Right now! Go over there and slap her!"

She started crying again and said, "Daddy, I don't know how to fight."

"Well, you going to learn today." I grabbed her by her shirt and pulled her closer to Aajani, but Aaniyah just stood there with her hands covering her face and tears running down her arms. I removed her hands from her face and confronted her with a low, growling, aggressive tone. "Listen to me; you're going to hit her, and you're going to do it now."

Aajani, with her arms folded, said, "She better not hit me!"

Filled with anger and hostility, I impulsively swung and backhanded Aajani across her face. She fell to the ground holding her cheek and looked at me with the greatest mistrustful eyes that I'd ever seen, started crying, and said, "Daddy, I'm sorry . . . I'll never hit her again, I promise."

At that moment, all I could do was stare at my hand because I couldn't believe that I'd lost control and hurt my daughter. I once made a promise to my children that I'd never hit them and gave them my oath. Bamm-Bamm also began to weep, she and Aaniyah were both sobbing asking for their mother. I reached down to pick Aajani up, but she cringed from my touch.

With the sincerest voice that I could muster, I said, "I'm sorry. It was an accident, sweetheart."

She then allowed me to pick her up, and while she was still crying she said, "Daddy, I thought you said you would never hit me."

I faced her, full of remorse, and gently touched both of her shoulders and said softly, "Baby, I'm sorry. I'm so sorry; I promise I'll never do it again."

She didn't say anything and continued weeping. Feeling self-abased about what I'd done, I got angry at myself and said, "Hit me!"

She looked at me with the biggest forgiving eyes and tears running down her face and said, "It's okay, Daddy."

"It's not okay! Hit me!" I demanded.

She shook her head. "No, Daddy, it's okay."

"I hurt you, and you forgive me that easy and tell me it's okay?"

"Yes," she replied.

I couldn't believe that she was so pardoning for my actions, and it hurt me deeply to get that type of warmth after what I'd done, and I said avidly, "No, I need you to hit me."

She said, "Please, Daddy, I don't want to. It's okay."

I lost it and went into a frenzy, shouting, "It's not okay! It's not okay! It's not okay! It's never okay!"

"Stop, Daddy, please! I'm scared!" she said.

I stopped moving around and looked at her and said, "You don't understand—something like that is never okay!"

She walked over to me and put her arms around my waist, held me tightly, and then looked up at me with tear-filled eyes and said, "Daddy, you don't want us anymore?"

I looked at her. "Why would you ask me that?" I said.

"You're not happy no more," she said, "and I think it's because of us."

I touched her face gently and said, "No, baby, it's not that at all, it's just that . . . your father is going through a lot right now and something is not right."

"What's not right, Daddy? What's wrong?"

I was verklempt and bit my bottom lip to fight back my emotions, but I was sea-deep into my feelings and could no longer control my tears from falling. As I wept, I told her, "I don't know."

She looked down and held me tighter. Everyone in the room was crying, so I motioned Aaniyah and Bamm-Bamm to come over, and I then lifted them up, one in each arm.

Aajani, with her head still on my chest, said, "I wish that I could build a time-traveling machine and take us back to the place where everything was much better so that our family could start over again. Because I miss the way things used to be; don't you too, Daddy?"

"Yes, I sure do sweetheart, more than anything," I told her.

We all stood in the middle of the room embracing, like a Hallmark moment, and then Aajani looked up at me and said, "Daddy, you can still find happiness again if you had some help. Can you get some professional help somewhere? Please, can you?"

I paused and stared at her for a while, and finally I said, "Sure, baby, I'll get some help."

She placed her head back on my chest and said, "Dad?"

"Yes, darling?"

"Can you help us too?"

"What do you need help with?" I asked her.

She looked back up at me and said, "Can you please shave your face and take a shower, because you look like the missing link and you have an odor that's following you around like Pepé Le Pew."

"Who, the skunk off Looney Tunes?" I asked.

"Yeah, Daddy," Bamm-Bamm said, "you smell like *fart!*"

The insult was embarrassing, but funny enough to make us all laugh. After the amusement at my expense, I knelt down and placed

Aaniyah and Bamm-Bamm back on the floor. I stood up and said, "How about if I helped y'all by getting you girls the Teacup Yorkie puppy that y'all always wanted?"

They shouted and jumped up and down, and Aaniyah said, "Can it be a girl so that we can name her Rocka?"

"Sure," I said, "y'all can name her whatever you like."

They started bouncing again and then Aajani stopped and said, "Hold up . . . so you're getting us a dog so that you don't have to clean yourself up?"

"No, silly, I'm still going to do that anyway, but thank you for shaming me."

With a sparkling smile on her face, as well as a hand on her hip as if nothing had happened. "You're welcome, Daddy. Anytime you need some constructive criticism, just let me know—I'm pretty good at it."

CHAPTER 13
REFRESHER

I needed an intercession to see how many licks it would take to get to the Tootsie Roll center of my Tootsie Pop, so I made a call to get myself some professional help. I contacted Dr. Zielinski's office and spoke to her secretary, who informed me that the earliest available appointment with the psychotherapist wasn't for another thirty days. Desperately, I expressed a sense of the semi-emergency nature of my call; however, she was only able to place me on a cancelation list, which meant my appointment would be only tentative.

A few days later, I was contacted by the assistant who said the doctor had a cancellation and the time slot was available. After volunteering, I didn't bother getting fancy for my visit and went to my appointment as I was. Dr. Zielinski greeted me and said, "You look better." I knew that was a damn lie because at that time, I hadn't even honored my daughter's hygiene request for a tidying intervention.

I stopped dead in my tracks and confronted her right on the spot. "Are you serious? Look at me . . . I look like I've been playing in dirt!"

"I apologize," she said. "I honestly had good intentions with my euphemism, so let me start over by asking why you need to see me."

I took a seat and said, "Since the last time I saw you, everything was going smooth; as a matter of fact, it was great—until my best friend, who was like a brother to me, killed himself. Then my fiancée—well, ex-fiancée—got pregnant, and to top that off, somebody is trying to kill me. I need to sleep but I can't, because I'm afraid to sleep. I've been feeling like one of those *Night of the Living Dead* zombies from that Michael Jackson *Thriller* video. Life couldn't possibly be any worse than this, and I just can't handle it. I desperately need your help!"

She looked at me and said, "Whew, forgive me, but um, where do we start? Okay, let's begin with why you're not able to sleep, because you definitely look like you haven't been getting any."

"Well," I told her, "when I am able to fall asleep, my dreams are gruesomely vivid and unforgettable."

"So tell me about them," she said.

"I have this reoccurring nightmare that my family is being tortured by someone, and when I get close to rescuing them, I fail. There are different particular things that I'll do to save them each time I dream, but all of my efforts fall short. The previous dream changes subtle details for the next, similar dream that I'll have, but the outcome is still the same, because this motherfucker still slaughters them the exact same way every single time! I'm sorry—excuse my language. But, it's like a sick butterfly effect inside of a dream."

"Is this person that's doing these things to your family someone you know?" she asked.

"Yes."

"Also, is this the same person who's trying to kill you?"

"I believe so," I answered.

She wrote some things down on a pad. "Okay, tell me about your friend who committed suicide."

"Well, he was going through a lot of issues with his marriage and employment after losing his job. The harder he tried to fix his problems, the worse things got for him. He needed immediate results, but time just wasn't on his side. He didn't just kill himself—he killed his wife too, and I feel horrible about it."

"Why?"

After a long pause, I said, "Because he came to my home earlier that day and spoke to me about his situation, and it was obvious that he was hurting. But I was useless because I wasn't able to tell him anything worthwhile or do anything to stop his pain. Before he left, he turned to me and said, 'Bro, never let me go.' And I just stood there like a fuckin' idiot. Not long after that, I received a call from him telling me that he loves me, and I knew something was wrong the way he said good-bye. Now it's eating me up, because it was only at that point is that I really tried to do something, but it was too late. I should've stopped him when I had the chance, so now all I can think about is how I let him go when he asked me not to. If I had just done something to help him when I had the opportunity, I could've saved them both. But I didn't, and I feel guilty about it."

She continued writing for a moment and then said, "Tell me about your relationship."

"Our relationship failed because the cumulative chaos left me kind of scatterbrained, and on top of that she got pregnant, and I wasn't thrilled about having another child in the midst of these circumstances. She insisted that we have the baby, but I made my position clear that I wasn't going to be supportive of her decision, so that led to the house of cards falling down."

She said, "Well, naturally I would tell you congratulations, but it's obvious that you're not too happy about it. But it does sound like you've been through a couple traumatic experiences, and from my observation of your physical condition and listening to your present state of affairs, it appears that you're suffering from a serious case of acute depression."

"So what do we do?" I said.

"You need to feel a sense of hopefulness," she said. "Do you have a higher power?"

"Why would you ask me that?"

"It's only a question," she said.

"Well, I don't, so now are you going to judge me and say I'm doomed if I don't believe in a God?"

"No," she answered. "Having a positive faith in something could be used as a tool, and it appears to have varying degrees of success with some of my patients. I'm a pantheist, so I believe in a higher power and not a personal God, but I am open-minded to those who do."

Irritated, I said, "Okay, let's move on. What am I supposed to do?"

She said, "Your perception is a very powerful, life-changing interface with the world. If you could optimistically change how you perceive your past experiences, or information about your current environment, you will consciously gravitate in the direction of pure clarity. We are physical avatars of our ideas, and we have the capability of redirecting any preconceived prejudices that we believed at one time were true, and the ability to remodel any undesirable traits about our personality that we wish to. Our all-encompassing perception about our entire life subconsciously defines who we are at any given time. A thorough, honest metacognitive evaluation of your perception will change your life indefinitely."

"Okay," I said, "what does all that mean?"

"The pain you feel is psychological. You're internalizing misery that was manifested externally. Don't allow yourself to become a prisoner with things from the past you cannot change. You can make a positive impact on your future, starting with your choices. When you feel incomplete, stop and ask yourself what's most important right now, and I'm sure that you know what the answer is—you are! Your peace of mind is golden and should always be your number-one top priority when you are mentally deficient. Try your best to live in the now. Get out there, and don't be afraid to be diverse and free like the wind, while investing in healthy things you've never tried before."

"That's easier said than done," I said.

"I'm also going to write you a referral for a consultation to see a psychiatrist for a medication evaluation regarding your insomnia and depression. This should be a refreshing, epic journey, so I'm going to need you to divorce all your troubles and become a proponent for change, and also to become conscientiously devoted to protecting your tranquility once you've acquired it, okay?"

"Sure," I said unenthusiastically.

Then she asked, "What kind of things do you like to do, or what interest do you have that's relaxing; that'll provide you with your very own private utopia right here on earth?"

I took a moment to think about it and said, "Well, I don't have any hobbies right now that I could think of that would help place me in that type of idealistic setting other than my family."

"Well for now, considering your current situation. We need something else more attainable, something therapeutic that you could independently provide for yourself and not have to depend on others to give you."

"Well," I said, "when I was a kid, to get away from the outside world when things around me were hectic, I used to enjoy writing science-fiction thrillers. I really loved it because it was an escape for me. It was like being able to dream while I was wide awake . . . therapeutic, even."

"Then that's what you need to do: start writing to occupy yourself, and keep scrawling even if you never allow anyone to read your imagination."

I gave that thought some review, and optimistically said, "Yes, that's exactly what I'm going to do. I believe you just solved all of my problems without individually addressing either one of them.

You are really good. I knew you had the answers, and I have to give it to you—you're like a master guru or something."

"Thank you, but you have always had the answers," she said. "I'm just trained to articulate a panacea to help you realize it, and that's why I get paid the big bucks."

I was able to smile and said, "You deserve it." I got up to shake her hand. "Can I please have another pair of those happy feet?"

Looking at me with a dull stare, she said, "What happened to the last pair I gave you?"

"My ornery-ass pit bulls got to them one day and ripped them to shreds. I tried my best to get them out of their mouths, but they just demolished them. I guess they just didn't like Bobby McFerrin's face, because it was a vicious attack."

"I didn't see any picture of any dogs on your Facebook page, and with all those pictures you got posted, I'm sure I would've seen at least one."

"I'm sorry, I lied," I admitted. "I don't have dogs—it was me. I won't do it again."

She squinted her eyes at me like she was about to hand down a sentence of corporal punishment and have me flogged like a disobedient farmhand. But she gave me clemency, walked over to the cabinet, reached inside, and handed me my second pair of happy feet with half a smile on her face.

CHAPTER 14
HYPERREALITY

The ruminating, inspirational pep talk from Dr. Zielinski resonated through every cell in my body and brilliantly emphasized the essence of nirvana. I also followed up on the consultation to see the psychiatrist she referred me to so that I could receive my pharmaceutical medications, which felt like happy pills. With the renewed spiritualism of a Zen Buddhist monk and the assistance of my medicinal concoction, I felt like I now owned the tools to scrutinize and rationalize anything philosophically. Through the process of deductive reasoning, I started syllogizing my personal bigotries with a thorough self-examination to free myself from every single antiquated, dogmatic ideology that I possessed. After performing the honest assessment, I discovered that I had a great deal of trivial hypocrisies that contaminated my values. I'm not sure why I audaciously perceived the ridiculous notion that I would be less than a man by sitting in a bathtub of water to wash my body. That unsound viewpoint illustrated a biased mindset, which expressed one of several foolish ideologies I'd subconsciously contracted somehow and infected me like an insidious disease. I couldn't believe that I actually carried the perception that something so frivolous would be a sacrilegious act for a man. No longer foolishly restrained from this luxury, I opened up the bathtub faucets and grabbed a thirty-two-ounce bottle of Morning Glory, made by the iconic Calgon brand. I emptied its contents into the cascade of water and then stood there, amazed, and watched the liquid turn into blue magic. After my fascination, I undressed and took the Calgon challenge of taking me away, by submerging my body into the deep-seated Jacuzzi of aquatic pleasures. Jet streams tickled my flesh, circulating the water into a whirlpool of multiplying transparent bubbles that resembled a cosmic galaxy. It felt like I was bathing in the celestial heaven surrounded by trillions of twinkling stars. I was proud of conquering a bizarre insecurity without shame, and I giggled loudly like a mischievous leprechaun who had just found his lucky pot of gold.

The reoccurring nightmares I was having also took a vacation, which subsequently provided me the therapeutic justice of some deep REM sleep that helped restore my overall vitality. My equilibrium was finally distributed equally throughout my entire body, and like the soul singer Patti LaBelle, I had a "new attitude," which I refused to let anything jeopardize. Cat and I were also on quasi-friendly terms, which wasn't my greatest expectation, but it opened up the space for us to have an amicable dialogue concerning our children's health and welfare.

One drizzling Saturday, I decided to initiate writing in a vapor of hearing the violent sounds of a storm's roaring thunder crack the sky, causing angry vibrations that shook my window pane. The ominous weather conditions inspired me to select a melodic piece of classical music as a theme for inspiration. I chose André Rieu's work "O Fortuna," which is an aesthetic masterpiece originally composed by Carl Orff in 1937. Together with the storm, the acoustic master blaster amalgamated a sublime, unadulterated axis-of-evil-ish sound that naturally encouraged the motif for my creativity. The elements surrounding me conjured up a deep, dark fantasy that rented a secret chamber inside my brain I'd never known to exist.

I grabbed a pen and a writer's notebook and began drafting while I paced the carpet with footsteps consistent with the musical composition. My writing hand was scribing my abstract thoughts fiendishly, and the blank sheets of paper were filling up just as quickly as I could turn the pages. I was amazed with this sudden, extraordinary ability that I seemed to acquire from nowhere to create a futuristic novella that had the potential of becoming a paradigm in the entire genre of science fiction. Then, nearly at the summit of my affair, I received a phone call that broke the line of communication between my linear visualization and my penmanship.

No longer mentally present in my creative-genius zone, I answered the call to hear Ronnie tell me that his Corvette broke down not far from my home and he was desperately in need of some vehicular assistance. I placed my one-of-a-kind, creative sci-fi work of art to the side and drove in the pouring rain to his aid.

We spent some time attempting to revive his vehicle in spite of the unforgiving weather before he eventually called a tow truck. While we waited together inside my truck for the recovery vehicle to arrive, to pass the time I challenged his perception on some sinister personal information about me that could be considered paradoxical.

I turned to him with a studious look on my face and said, "Bro, I need to ask you something."

I could tell I got his undivided attention when he said, "What's up?"

I told him that I needed him to be very honest with me. "All right, I can do that," he said.

"Do you think I'm crazy?" I asked him.

"No."

"Do you believe that you're crazy?"

Emphasizing his answer with an arched eyebrow, he said, "Hell no."

Now that I had his immutable answers, I superimposed my thesis on him. "I think it's time I tell you something about me that you didn't know: I'm *crazy* as hell. And so are you!"

Ronnie blinked his eyes, shook his head, and looked at me like Scooby Dooby Doo. "I don't see any rationale in your theory. Elaborate, or give me something to substantiate your philosophy."

"All right," I said, "put your seatbelt on, because I'm about to take you on a fantastic voyage. People see me and think I'm a pretty logical guy who's well assembled and soundly put together, but no one knows that I think like a ravenous animal underneath this facade. The perception that I emit is an illusion, my language and mannerisms are a master disguise orchestrated to be accepted in my communal setting. To be truthful, I'm predatory, and I have some deranged thoughts that I would never tell you or anyone else because I would be characterized as being crazy."

He looked off and said, mockingly, "Man, that ain't nothing but evil lurking." Then turned back to me and declared, "All you need is some holy water."

"Now, that expression is cliché as fuck, it makes me think you actually *believe* that corny truism. See, let me tell you something . . . we've forgotten who we are, and evil is the classification the supercilious human beings prefer to blame when the instinctive, animalistic true nature of our primitive instinct reveals itself. When we hurt each other, it's just as natural as when any other species in the animal kingdom does it. You can't fool me. I know that you have those untamed, beastly thoughts too . . . come on, you can tell me."

Ronnie laughed and said, "Motherfucker, I'm not crazy!"

"It's nothing to be ashamed of," I said, "and you don't have to pretend that you're not crazy too for the sake of being afraid to lose your grip on reality. The entire compos mentis populace is naive to the fact that they're subconsciously pretending to be normal in what we have designed as a sophisticated monkey see, monkey do society. But ironically, we're all beasts born with embryonic, uncontrollable thoughts that we don't discuss with others because we don't want to alarm anyone. I want you to remember back when you were misbehaving as a juvenile delinquent, not acting accordingly."

"All right," he said.

"Do you ever recall you parents telling you, 'Boy . . . you better act like you have some sense.'"

"Yeah, a few times."

I balled up my fist, and with a hammering motion, I said, "Booyah! That's it! The key word is *act*. We've been conditioned since birth to be actors."

He squinted his eyes and simply replied, "Hmm."

I got the impression that he finally thought my theory had some logic, so I looked around, then leaned toward him to convey what I had to say next in a secretive deportment as if it was classified, I said, "Listen, our saneness is a conspiracy theory." I rested back in my seat before continuing. "Can you imagine what kind of consequences will befall someone for exposing and revealing this information? It's social suicide that will inevitably sabotage and annihilate a person's livelihood. So it's in the best interest of the wise to keep quiet about their psychological status."

At that very moment, I received a phone call from Cat, which impeded us from furthering our discourse about the topic. She asked me if I could pick Aajani up from her best friend's house and drop her off at her residence. When I questioned her availability, she reported that she was in the middle of providing her hair a deep-conditioning treatment and didn't want to leave her place with a damp mane. I verbalized a willingness to appease and informed Ronnie that I had to leave; we agreed to follow up on the interesting subject at a better and more convenient time. He hopped out of my vehicle and got inside of his own to wait on the tow truck.

The storm had subsided by the time I picked up my daughter. As soon as she entered my vehicle, she started yapping about her vivacious girlie life of sugar, spice, and everything nice. I pretended to show her acknowledgement with eye contact and head nods, even occasionally throwing in single-vowel conversation fillers for effect whenever I subconsciously gave her feedback. Little did she know, she was having this graphic conversation with herself. But I was having a very intimate, dialectical exchange with myself as well. I was still very much intrigued about my condition, and I began to explore more deeply into the reason why my unfavorable desires were inescapable.

During a brief moment of discerning my insoluble, demented state, I grew more and more confident in my philosophical realm until I peaked and hit the mother lode of discoveries. My emotions at that point were grandiloquent, comparable to how the Vatican would feel if it were to unearth the antiquitous Holy Grail. I identified that my animalistic thoughts and urges were organically primal, and had been nurtured inside my DNA since my embryonal conception. With the self-assurance of this piece of datum being culpable, I made a diagnosis on my sanity like a licensed physician sworn to the Hippocratic Oath and declared myself undoubtedly, absolutely crazy. But not in a clinical sense, however; more on a quasi-psychotic, superficial level because of my ability to manage it. The only traits that I possessed that separated me from the crazies in the insane asylum were empathy, which allowed me to have compassion for the next individual, and austerity, which provided me the self-discipline to operate in lockstep with a proper society. However, the worth of those precious traits was only as strong as my morality that gives them value, which appears at times to be worthless, because the core of my existential presence was always craving and begging for violence. Therefore, those fragile qualities were paramount in the distinction between the so-called crazies and the ill-informed, arrogant people who have been brainwashed to believe a sane mind is natural. I felt enlightened and ecstatic to be aware of our egregious, ingrained human social behaviors and to fully understand the real reason my cerebrum was preoccupied with madness. It was disturbing and empowering to know that I had the discretion to cause mass devastation on an unprecedented scale or to become the world's greatest philanthropic hero that ever lived. But something was not right, because I had this dual-personality complex inside that wanted to achieve both extremes. Until I'd made the decision about the direction of my destiny, it behooved me to remain adequately disciplined to fictitiously maneuver and function unnoticed within our fragile societal interior walls, so that I could effectively blend in homogenously with the misdirected Homo sapiens.

Right at that moment, on the brink of a complete parcel of ideas being packaged and shipped by FedEx with a signature authorization for me to accept an enclosed diploma, which certified and validated that I had been institutionalized by society to behave accordingly, an extraneous voice seeped into my conscious.

"Dad! Dad! Earth to Daddy!"

"Huh?"

"Why are you sitting like that in front of Mama's house?"

With my hands tightly gripping the steering wheel, I looked down and realized I was stiff as a board on the edge of my seat, sitting like a slew-footed chauffeur understudy for *Driving Miss Daisy*.

So I started fidgeting my legs and erroneously told her, "Oh, it's because I have to pee."

Cat came out of her home to show the world that she was clearly in her second trimester of pregnancy, and she gave me a polite wave. Aajani rolled down her window and yelled, "Mom, Dad has to pee-pee really bad—can he use the bathroom?"

With her hand still in the air, she signaled me an approval. "Sure, tell him to come in." Aajani got out of the vehicle, and I followed behind with my production of walking like an impersonating gimp, playing the role of a mediocre actor operating under the deception of a full bladder.

When I came out of the restroom, Cat told me that she'd just finished cooking dinner and asked if I'd like to stay and eat with them. I was surprised at the offer, and the kids appeared to be very excited about me staying. It was intuitive for me to interpret her gesture as an extended olive branch, so I reciprocated the proposal, saying, "Of course."

The children and I sat down at the dinner table while Cat served up a suggestive meal that had all the ingredients of a possible reunification. While we masticated our food, I asked Cat about how her day went. She placed her utensil down, therefore I knew this answer was going to be a long one.

"Well, since you asked, let me tell you. Do you remember that girl named Felicia that works with me?"

"The one with gold teeth from Memphis, Tennessee?"

"Yes," she said. "Let me tell you what her ghetto ass said to a patient today."

At that moment, I willingly disconnected with the conversation and visually transported to the enigmatic sci-fi project I was previously working on at home. I drifted into my cerebral arcade of intrepid adventures, dressed in a khaki uniform, and plunged deep inside the mysterious rabbit-hole-of-the-unknown, like Indiana Jones. Even though I was physically present, watching Cat's expressive figure like she was an animatronic Muppet, I couldn't hear the slightest sound. I was too busy masterfully crafting an ineffable scene too bizarre to be ordinary, even more so in the volatile world of the science-fiction industry. Without any degree of limitation in this abstract universe where anything could happen, I escorted myself effortlessly into the extremities of my narrative thriller.

All of a sudden, a shooting star smashed into my face and jerked me out of my intangible universe. Immediately, I became coherent and realized that the object wasn't a meteorite; it was a dinner roll that one of the kids had thrown across the table, which had hit me square in the center of my forehead.

Just then, Cat finished her storyline and said, "Can you believe that?"

Unaware of anything she'd chattered about up that point, I shook my head and responded, "She's stupid!"

After we finished dinner, Cat asked if I'd like to stay and watch *Curse of Chucky* with her after she put the children to bed. It was obvious that I appeared to be on the road of redemption for her to suggest us spending one-on-one time together, so I strongly obliged. I moved over to the comfortable sofa, got reacquainted with my previous thoughts, and resumed my chronicle while she got the children prepared for bedtime.

Cat ultimately disturbed my voyage with her reappearance, plopped down next to me, and said, "Okay, I just got finished reading the kids their bedtime story after brushing their teeth and putting on their pajamas, so are you ready to get this movie started?"

I smiled and said, "Sure." But I was mentally absent for the first half of the movie and truant from the random conversations she and I supposedly had, because I was still busy with my own cinematic thriller with ultramodern special effects included. There were some mind-blowing innovative technological concepts I toyed with that redefined the very laws of physics. Suddenly, I became morbidly frightened and my fantastic world went topsy-turvy. Somehow, I had inadvertently cross-contaminated my project with the previous "I know I'm crazy" rhetoric I'd had with Ronnie earlier. With that dynamic combination, I came to the realization that I had been remotely controlled by extraterrestrials from their galactic command center from outer space. I got the heebie-jeebies and started hyperventilating as discreetly as I could, because I didn't want to attract attention. I looked over at Cat, and she was intensely involved in the movie and even forespoke what she believed was going to happen next.

Just in case I was overdramatizing my mental screenplay, I stood up and pretended to adjust my clothes as a smokescreen for autocorrecting my stability. Then I sat back down to scrutinize my reality, but I had gone too far and there was no turning back from what I'd discovered. I realized that I'd just tapped into the true reality that people who've been erroneously committed into psych wards for being crazy knew. I panicked because it was too excruciating to accept that I wasn't in control and that everything I'd ever experienced had been predetermined and observed without my consent.

Before having a histrionic outburst in front of Cat, I excused myself under the false pretense of needing to use the restroom. I entered the lavatory under extreme duress and anxiously stripped nude, as if I was the star performer on a pornographic movie set in Bangkok Thailand. Once fully stripped, I began searching rigorously for the implanted Trojan horse surveillance bug with my ten digits, but I was unable to locate any monitors without the use of electronic counter-surveillance equipment. I slapped my face and told myself to pull it together, while I futilely watched my pitiful, depraved mind slip into the abyss of my two intertwined tales. I heard Cat in the distance yelling for me to hurry up, so I gave myself a pep talk while donning my clothing before exiting the restroom.

As I headed down the corridor to enter the living area, I passed my daughters' open room, glanced at them as they slept, and told myself, *that's what you're about to lose if you check out.* The fabric of the idea of not being around for my children disturbed me and increased my anxiety, and I couldn't falsify my instability when I rejoined Cat in the living room.

She asked me what was wrong because I was breathing heavily, like a locomotive choo-choo train. I seized the couch and sat next to her for a sense of security and said, "I can't breathe!"

"What were you doing in the bathroom—jumping jacks?"

"Cat, that's not funny. Why would I be in your bathroom exercising?"

"I don't know," she said, "but it's obvious that you can breathe because you're talking. What you mean is, you're having a difficult time breathing."

I grabbed my chest and said, "I need your help. Just tell me what to do."

She then told me to relax and concentrate on a deep-breathing technique. Acknowledging her professional recommendation, I reclined on the sofa in a more relaxed position and began breathing slowly. But the technique didn't work because my heart was pounding as though Grambling State University and Southern University marching bands were facing-off with each other at the Bayou Classic Battle of the Bands. I looked down at my chest, noticed my hand was physically jumping up and down like a drum major was conducting a performance off of Lil Jon's "Turn Down for What" song. Looking over at Cat, I said, "Feel my heartbeat."

She placed her hand on my chest and said, "Oh my goodness, why is your heart beating so fast? What the hell were you doing in the bathroom, Michael?"

I said, "I don't want to talk about it."

"Were you in there masturbating? Because we had a guy who came into the hospital the other day with heart palpitation from doing the exact same thing and he—"

I cut her off before she could complete her anecdote and said, "Hell no, I wouldn't make a porno crime scene out of your bathroom, and besides, you don't have any smut magazines in there. Why in the hell are we talking about perverted shit anyway? My fuckin' heart rate is out of control!"

"Well, I need to figure out what precipitated your irregular heartbeat," she said.

"Trust me, it's not that."

"All right," she said. "I need you to continue to do like I told you, so relax and concentrate on controlling your breathing at a slow, steady rhythm, and let's try to get through this movie."

"Cool," I agreed.

Then, I tried to disassociate myself from the gnarly revelation by *parlaying* back into the recliner and coordinate my vitals. But my attempts were still futile, because I was too deeply infested with malaise to overcome my ordeal with relaxation. Besides, we were watching a hideous, unnatural murdering doll that was cleverly sentient, executing precision signature kills. I thought, *this butcher is supposed to be an inanimate object, so how is it possible he's capable of having mechanics?* I began to entertain the idea that nothing was untouchable from being remotely controlled from a distant source; anyone could be a suspect—even my family.

Considering my last assumption being a strong probability, I glanced over at Cat with suspicion and cruised up-and-down her form with an eagle eye. I continued my examination, until I became disheartened about the inkling and tried to shake it off. Struggling with my conflictive realities, I needed positive encouragement to give me the strength to put my thoughts into perspective. So I reached out for inspiration, then began reciting in my head a notable quotation from Martin Luther King's speech. *"I have a dream that one day, little black boys and girls will be holding hands with little white boys and girls . . ."* That motivational sermon by the late civil-rights leader inspired me to become a world-class champion Sloppy Joe eater, by consuming a record number of them in an hour. I was sure the feat would earn me a top spot in the *Guinness Book of World Records.* Then I thought, *what the hell does either one of those have to do with each other or my situation—MLK's era was before I was born, and I don't even like Sloppy Joes.* I was surely losing my marbles. My thoughts were like scrambled eggs in a skillet of misperception, and I consciously told myself to stop thinking, so that I could attempt to keep my sanity altogether. But, an inactive mind was hard to accomplish as Chuckie continued his relentless murdering spree; the violent activities in the movie were too over-the-top for me to cope with, which perpetuated my fears. It was necessary for me to convince Cat to get this maniacal killing doll off the screen ASAP and to find something dolce for my condition.

"Cat, I have to tell you something." She paused the movie and gave me her attention.

"Lately, I've been working real hard on a project at the house and have been occupied with it mentally since I've been here, and I can't take it because it's driving me crazy."

She stared at me and didn't say a word, until I said, "Did you hear me? I'm not able to escape it and I'm losing my sanity right now as I speak!"

"So you're telling me that you've been thinking of other stuff and ignoring me the entire time you've been here?"

Oh my goodness, I thought, *I'm a basket case who's about to be admitted into an insane asylum and meet new friends who want to slobber on me, or worse, die from a heart attack in two motherfuckin' minutes, and that's what you say?*

But what actually came out of my mouth was, "Listen, I have an incredible problem right now that's much worse than me ignoring you. This is an astronomical problem. I've just come to the metaphysical realization of what's going on with everyone, and I'm very afraid right now because I can't handle what I know. It's inconceivable and complicated, but I can explain it to you in a way that you will understand. Would you like to know what's going on?"

"Hell no!" she said.

"All right, but can you please turn off that movie because that doll is doing some things that's not natural, and I need to watch something softer."

She appeased me by substituting what we were watching to an episode of *Family Guy*. I said, "Thanks, this is much better. I need to focus on this cartoon to take my mind off what's going on. I just need to laugh." But my lame attempt to force laughter at something that wasn't funny was even more disturbing, especially when I noticed that Peter Griffin had testicles for a chin. I thought, *he actually has sex organs on his face . . . that's not practical, why in the hell would they do that.* Then one of the animated characters' head exploded, with blood splattering everywhere. I launched off the sofa like a rocket and shouted, "Turn this shit off!"

Cat was startled at my outburst, quickly turned the television off, and said, "What's wrong?" Her question went unanswered when a feeling of vertigo came over me, so I told her I needed to lie down because I was dizzy. I got on the floor in a supine position and silently watched the ceiling fan cyclone in a continuous motion. Cat stood over me, confused about how to further help me, her disposition was stoic because she couldn't understand what was going on. Then she said, "I think I should call an ambulance."

"No," I said, "just play something soothing for me to listen to and get me some water, please." I desperately needed something to defocus my attention from the dire, inevitable doom I was facing and reorganize a healthier, serene atmosphere that would be more beneficial to my stability.

Cat grabbed her iPod and played the Berlin song "Take My Breath Away." The calming melody of the ballad pacified me until I heard the chorus. I said to myself, *why would people write a song like this? I don't want my breath taken away.* I knew right then it was the outside entity sending me a message through a song that they were going to murder me through asphyxiation so there would be no trace of their involvement. I imploded, and my freak-out escalated to ten point zero on the Richter scale. I was exceedingly hot, and lava seemed to course through my veins. My internal organs felt like a cataclysmic earthquake setting off a massive volcanic eruption. I was so desperate to cool my body temperature and avoid hyper-thermal shock that I would've guzzled antifreeze with a funnel shoved down my esophagus if it were suggested. My heartbeat severely resumed its pulsating alertness with every accelerated beat, alarming a repetitive message of *Danger! Danger! Danger!* I catapulted off the floor and snatched the bottle of water from Cat's hand as I headed toward the restroom, because even the content in my intestine was terrified and started its decline down an escape tube to abandon an allegorical burning building. I made it to the restroom and sat on the toilet just in time before my waste bravely jumped into the porcelain catch net. While I sat on the commode huffing and puffing, I began sweating profusely when an unquenchable desire for aqua became urgent. Quickly twisting the top off the bottled water, I started gulping like a *water-a-holic* and saved a portion to pour on top of my head because my skull felt like a nuclear reactor.

After my sphincter signaled the closing of my orifice, I snatched some ass tissue and wiped the lingering excrements of my cowardly buddy's successful evacuation down my intestinal escape tunnel. Before I flushed, I stood up, and I considered looking down at my waste to see if everything was normal. But I reconsidered that notion because I fretted about the idea of my feces having facial recognition, with huge blinking eyeballs and tiny hands waving "Goodbye, sucker."

Before I left the restroom, I wanted to say something encouraging in an attempt to pull myself together. I stood in front of the mirror, staring at myself, and started soliloquizing. "You will be okay, all right."

Then a stranger interrupted me with a strong voice and said, "No you won't."

I pivoted around a full three hundred and sixty degrees looking for the perpetrator, but I didn't see anyone else inside the bathroom except for my reflection. Since I was the only one present, I figured the suspect was inside my head, so I gripped the sink and eyeballed my likeness and said, "Who are you?"

"It's me." the voice said.

"Who is me?" I asked. Then I heard a rumbling laugh, and I said, "Why are you doing this to me?"

The voice toyed with me and mimicked what I said in a sardonic tone, saying, "Why are you doing this to me?"

"This isn't funny." I said.

The voice continued to tease me in a self-satisfying, condescending nature and said, "Yes it is."

"Stop it!" I said.

"You can't make me."

Then the restroom began to close in on me as phantasmagorical figures developed from nothing, and invaded my enclave. Fearful, I reached down and pulled out my pistol from my ankle holster, cocked it, and placed the gun to my head. I looked my reflection in the eye, and I yelled, "Leave me the fuck alone!"

Suddenly, everything stopped. Just for a moment, I wavered about my decision to pull the trigger, but I kept the gun firmly pressed against my temple because I wasn't sure if the agonizing threat was terminated. After some quietude provided me assurance it was over, I placed my weapon back inside the holster and said, "I need to get the fuck out of here!"

I exited the rickety panic room and entered the hallway, and it appeared altered, as if it was elongated from what I remembered. I was thunderstruck, body mechanics stiff with fear. "Oh, shit, now I'm in the *Twilight Zone!*" Silently, I questioned myself, asking, *what if I did commit suicide inside that bathroom, and now I'm about to enter another dimension of otherworldly, amorphous beings?* I was frightened of being consciously aware of the idea. "Oh no, not that . . . this can't be real!" I said. Then I began to challenge and question the validity of what was really real and the true essence of the term. I touched myself and said, "What if I'm not real, or my family was never real?" I gasp at the cognitive acceptance, and made a silent theorization, *"Everything that I'd ever experienced appears to be material in our infantile psychology. But in actuality, our reality is a fantasy, with no physical merit. This world is an emotional hologram on a fabrication of continuous time projected to us in a dioramic format. Realism is a placebo ingeniously designed by a dominant, super-intelligent extraterrestrial source. We're inside a multifaceted game console that has a hierarchy of multiple layers, and even though it's consciously inescapable . . . we have a silver lining to our predicament. Because someday, we'll master our simulated universe by finding the unambiguous be-all and end-all algorithm to turn science into magic and undoubtedly play God ourselves.*

Standing in the same spot and waiting on a self-realized intervention, I thought again, *man, you really need to pull it together pronto. What's the likelihood of some bullshit like that happening?* Then, for some ill-fated reason, I thought about the movie *The Matrix*. I shook my head and said aloud, "Whoa, I'm fucked!"

Something isn't right, I thought. *I must be lucid dreaming or something.* Considering everything that was going on was so bizarre and surreal, I believed that just maybe I could wake myself up with a fairytale-induced sorcerous trick. Closing my eyes, I thought of the movie *The Wizard of Oz*, and wished upon a star that I had Dorothy's magically bedazzled shoes on my feet. Clicking my heels together, I said, "There's no place like home." I opened my eyes and looked down and saw I was barefoot. "Damn."

I decided to hurry up and get it over with, so like a lone Spartan pitted against the entire Persian army, I slapped my chest repeatedly until I built up the momentum to face my crucible. At that point, I began my locomotion by humming a pugilistic cadence with the zeal of a formidable warrior down the aisle of the unknown. My heart was shooting rapid fire with a rat-a-tat-tat tempo like a Thompson submachine gun, because I knew beneath the surface of my bravado, if the room I was entering wasn't exactly the way I remembered, I would go into shock trauma like a dysfunctional war veteran and crash and burn on sight. But I overcame my fear en route by pumping myself up and asking, *what would Leonidas do?*

When I breached the threshold, I shouted, "This is Sparta!" Then I realized that Cat was the only individual in the room, sitting on the sofa reading a book.

She looked up, acknowledged me, and said, "Why are you in character, acting like you're auditioning for the movie *300?*"

I was breathing rapidly because of my anticipation, but I chose not to say anything about my entrance because I was embarrassingly speechless, and I dropped my guard then she asked me with a greater concern, "Baby, are you okay?"

I was relieved to know I was still in the dimension that I was familiar with, at least from my observation, as far as I could tell. Still doubtful, I knew everyone who appeared to exist would be suspect anyway. Nevertheless, I didn't want to draw any more attention nor did I choose to interrogate her about her suspicious existence, so I adjusted my bearings and confidently said, "Yeah, but I need to go."

She stood up and got a closer look at me and said, "You're drenched. Did you take a shower with your clothes on?"

"Something like that," I said, then grabbed my shoes and put them on.

"How about, you spending the night here with us?" Cat said.

"Maybe next time," I told her. "I have something important to take care of in the morning, and I need to go home to prepare."

She gave me a hug; I took advantage of her closeness and started squeezing her to make sure she was real. She said, "Stop—you're squeezing me too hard. What are you doing?"

I said, "I haven't touched you in a while, and I just wanted to make sure your fruit was still fresh."

"Okay," she said, "you're scaring me a little bit. Are you sure you're all right?"

I tried to look as genuinely credible as possible and nodded my head. "Yeah."

We then said good-bye to each other, and I headed to my paper castle.

I pulled up to the front of my home and surveyed its assembly while still inside my vehicle, looking for a contrast or any glitches in the system that would alert me to a devised set-up. I detected no nuanced variation from what I remembered, so I exited my starship and instantly looked up to make sure the sky wasn't falling. Walking briskly towards the front door, I thought, *man, Chicken Little was way before his time, he tried to warn us a long time ago, but no one would listen.*

CHAPTER 15
THE CRUCIBLE

I entered my home with a suspicious attention to detail, but I soon acknowledged that everything was still in place just like I'd left it. I immediately entered the kitchen and pulled out my medicine to calm my jitters. It was no secret to me that my cerebral databank had short-circuited and somehow I had mysteriously developed an unusual defect in my software, which allowed me to be consciously aware of the system. The systemic, failsafe protocol rendering me a rambling, unintelligible clinical crazy was a failure, for the reason that I was still fully aware and consciously sane and sound, which made me a threat to the operator's mainframe. I was a defective model with nonstandard behavior; surely, they had been alerted to this anomaly, and it was an imminent modus operandi for my components to be evaluated, which without a doubt would lead to a mandatory software reset to factory mode or an inevitable liquidation of my central processing unit. It would be too risky to allow a renegade automaton model who possesses intellectual awareness to corrupt the other unknowing contestants with a virus-like sentience.

After I was able to get my heart rate under control with the help of my medication, it was time for me to strategize and construct a plan to circumvent capture, because I knew they were coming. But before I could formulate my strategy, I heard vehicles screeching to a halt in front of my house. I rushed into Valhalla to retrieve my twelve-gauge pistol-grip shotgun, ran into my bedroom, and hid in my closet for concealment. I began breathing heavily from the excitement, and my heart was galloping like champion racehorse Seabiscuit going for the Triple Crown. At the same time, I sensed a burning sensation of liquid oozing out of my chest. "Oh shit, my heart has combusted . . . now it's bleeding."

  I reached up and grabbed my left pectoral, expecting to feel a considerable amount of blood percolating through my pores and saturating my shirt, but all I felt was a fistful of rapid, pulsating thumps to indicate that my heart was in fight-or-flight mode. Relieved it was a false alarm, I continued to huddle with my defensive firearm and await their entry to confiscate their property.

  After some time of nervously waiting in the dark with no sign or indication of an anticipated extraction, I started to feel claustrophobic in the tight space and came out of the safe room. I began sweeping my home again with my weapon in tow for any indication of the intruder's presence. With no more rooms to check, I stood in the center of my living room feeling somewhat victorious until I was thrown off balance after having an eye-opener. I finally realized that my situation was inescapable, and my home was actually the insane asylum that housed me. Discovering who was behind the curtains pulling the strings to this fantasy world I once thought to be reality was a surreal moment that left me hopeless. It was crushing after I surrendered to the supposition that I couldn't possibly win or be triumphant against an immutable machine that had designed the very world around me. Euthanasia was the only solution to any form of solace for my mind to rest in peace, so I began to reminisce about the happier times with my family when things were simple and plain as a final tribute.

Undeniably, after that muted moment I couldn't help but think that I'd had a better quality of life when I lived in ignorance and traveled with the unsuspecting herd of sheep on the imaginary trail of reality. Education along with awareness of sensitive information can be a double-edged sword; it's detrimental, and should be a crime to obtain certain knowledge. I'd gone too far with my inquisitive nature and found out the riddle of life, which I knew at that moment was the ultimate taboo. Now that my game was over, I had to pay the piper. I felt a tsunami of anguish when I exhaled my last breath of hope; I was being methodically tormented beyond my max, and I wanted it stopped permanently. It was too excruciating to endure suffering any longer, so I decided to tap out.

I walked over to my desktop computer and pulled out a sheet of paper from the printer, got myself a pen, and wrote, "I'm sorry. I love you," with a signature on my final declaration to validate for my loved ones that it was me. Nearly lifeless, I stood in front of the nineteenth-century Victorian mirror hanging on the wall in the living room and then cocked my weapon before I placed it underneath my chin. I looked at the man behind the mirror and said calmly, "This is what you want, right?" Closing my eyes, I took one last deep breath with my finger on the trigger and then I heard *Boom! Boom! Boom!*

Something uninvited was beating on my door with monkey knuckles at three o'clock in the morning. After ruling out the possibility that it might have been the local Girl Scout troop promoting my favorite minty thin cookies, I took precaution and went into defense mode and crept to the door with the twelve-gauge shotgun. I looked through the peephole, and it was Ronnie. I said, "What you want, bro?"

He said, "I just came by to check on you. Open up."

"How did you know I was home?" I asked.

"Well, this life-size Tonka truck isn't invisible, especially when you drive over street signs, leaving tire evidence that leads up to it. Besides, you're parked on top of your lawn. So the scene out here kind of snitched on your whereabouts."

I thought that he had a good point, but I was positive that he was an operative impersonating a familiar face to bamboozle me into a trap to capture me.

"You shouldn't be popping up like a jack-in-the-box at this hour . . . I'm okay," I said.

"Cat called me and asked me to come by and check on you."

"How do I know it's you?" I said.

"Ronnie" paused for too long, so I said, "That's what I thought. Go away, man."

He then said, "Remember that time we were racing our motorcycles and you pulled that daredevil stunt, but that semi-truck came close to knocking your block off, and you *shitted* all over yourself?"

I said, "I beat you, though."

"That's right," he said, "you *did* beat me. But who else other than your brother would know you got a weak gut? I had to smell your backdraft all the way back home."

I thought, *yeah, that's highly top-secret information; he has to be the real deal.* Still, with my weapon at my side, I opened the door cautiously.

He came inside, looked at me, and said, "I told you it was me. Why are you answering the door with that big-ass rocket launcher? What you got going on?"

As we walked toward the living room with me in the lead, I fibbed about a previous break-in as an excuse. "We just had a burglary in our area about a week ago, and I heard some noise not too long ago, so I just wanted to be safe."

He said, "I noticed some teenagers drag racing their cars in your neighborhood when I pulled up. The kids are harmless—they're just having a little late-night fun—like we used to."

Without looking at him, I said, "Oh, okay."

He said, "Look at me, because I need to ask you something serious."

I looked at him and welcomed his question with a silent expression. "That conversation we had earlier concerns me about your sanity," he said, "so I need you to be straight up with me and tell me if there's something wrong."

I didn't want to circumvent my condition when he could clearly see through me like cellophane, and it was all too apparent that something wasn't right. I was nervous about what I desperately needed to ask him, but I bit my bottom lip and asked, "Are you really real? You're not a hologram, are you?"

"I'm not a hologram, and yes I'm real," Ronnie answered.

I got aggravated and yelled, "How in the *fuck* do you know?"

He calmly extended both of his arms out like he was preparing to get frisked by a patrolman and pivoted around until he reached a full three hundred and sixty-degree turn, faced me, and said, "Look at me, bro; here, come and touch me."

I walked over closer to him and reached out to touch his arm, and he double-crossed me by snatching my weapon out of my other hand.

I got upset and yelled, "Give me my goddamn weapon back!"

He stepped back with my twelve-gauge shotgun down by his side and said, "I can't do that. This is for your own safety."

"You're going to give me back that rifle." I demanded.

"You just going to have to fight me for it, bro."

"Motherfucker, you better give me back my gun right now before I crush you!"

Ronnie just stood there and made no attempt to give me back the weapon, so I said, "You're out of time."

I approached him to pulverize him into the million laser pixels it took to make his three-dimensional image, but he countered my intentions by drawing up the weapon and pointing the barrel at my face. His self-protective action caused me to stop in my tracks. But I was still furious and shouted, "You think I'm scared? Pull the goddamn trigger . . . hurry up and do it now! If you don't, I'm going to beat the dog shit out of you and then I'm going to murder your punk ass, because none of this shit is real anyway."

Still pointing the gun at me, he said, "Listen bro, I'm not the enemy, all right! We already lost one brother, and I don't want to lose you too. Trust me . . . we can work this out; I'll give you back the gun right now, if you can relax."

I just stood there huffing and puffing like a high-performance racecar with a Flowmaster muffler exhaust kit for lungs. I felt insecure without my gun, so I tried calming my aggression to trick him into giving it back to me. He took the bait after he saw that I was relaxed and then he backed up and lowered the weapon, discharging all five slugs that I had inside the chamber and placing them into his pocket. He gave me some crapola story to justify stealing my ammo, saying, "I'm only temporarily holding these, and you can have them back once we figure out what's going on."

At that point, he handed me back an empty weapon. However, I had more slugs in my armory, so I told him, "You can have 'em . . . now get out of my house."

He shook his head and said, "Man, I don't know what been going on with you, but ever since y'all moved into this house, you haven't been the same."

"It's because I get degenerate guests like you, so get the fuck out!" I yelled.

He threw his hands up as an act of passivity and said, "Okay, I'll leave, just let me get some water before I go because this situation got me dehydrated." I didn't say anything as he walked into the kitchen. He came back into the living room with my bottles of medication in his hand and said, "I didn't know you were taking trazodone and fluoxetine; how long you been on these prescriptions?"

"What difference does it makes? I told you all ready to get the fuck out of my house."

He approached me aggressively and said, "I'll fuckin' tell you what difference it makes. These psychoactive drugs that you're taking are the reason why you have lost your goddamn mind!"

I looked at him like he was an extraterrestrial from somewhere out there in planetary nebula and said, "What the hell you talking about?"

He said, "Five years ago, my aunt was battling severe postpartum depression and suffering from insomnia, so she went to her long-term doctor and his insidious ass gave her the exact prescriptions that you have right here. Guess what happened next? Within six months, she killed herself by blowing her fuckin' brains out in front of my niece."

I just looked at him without saying anything until he asked me for the name of the doctor who prescribed me the medicines. I told him the full name of my physician who had his own private practice. To my surprise, Ronnie recited the physical address of the office building, including the suite number, as if he'd had it memorized. "How you know that?" I asked.

"That's Doctor Death, who prescribed the exact same drugs that murdered my auntie." he told me.

I was convinced that he knew who my doctor was, but I was skeptical about the medicinal precursor he was trying to link to his aunt's suicide and said, "Bullshit!"

"Come here," he said, "I want to show you something." He led me to the computer and Googled both of the prescriptions and scrolled to the section that listed a plethora of side effects that I was unaware of. The downside of the first medicine was adverse psychiatric symptoms associated with my current experiences: mania, paranoia, delirium, agitation, psychosis, hallucinations, and self-destructive behavior. The side effects of the second medication consisted of fast, irregular heartbeat; increased sweating;

increased thirst; irritability; hostility; and suicidal ideation. My reaction to the information was so paralyzing that I heard two thuds hitting the floor: the first sound from me dropping my weapon, and the other was my lower jaw bottoming-out. I was in awe of this exposure.

Ronnie saw my reaction and said, "Yeah, bro, your reality is distorted and your perception has been deceived by the medication you're taking. They weakened your ability to function with a lucid mind, and made you susceptible to insanity."

I picked up the bottles and said, "Wow, I never thought to look at the side effects of these drugs. Why would our government allow the pharmaceutical companies to produce these medications and issue them to the public?"

He said, "You have to understand that it all boils down to the bottom line . . . which is economics and politics. The Food and Drug Administration can't stop the collaborators so they mandate them to list the side effects as a warning, and a lot of people *do* receive relief from their condition without any obvious signs of distress. But there are also a lot of people who are naive and oblivious about the dangers, or know about the repercussions of the drugs and still don't care. Regardless of anyone's necessity for taking them, just like any other pleasure principle, they more or less come with a price. My family has been greatly affected by this malpractice tragedy. Currently we're involved in a class-action lawsuit with a lot of other families across the nation with a prestigious law firm that has validated that these pharmaceutical drug companies are in cahoots with our government, which is responsible for an astounding number of negligent deaths. It's no ancient Chinese secret that these Fortune 500 drug cartels use lobbyists to approach our politicians with promises, favors, and payoffs, which they don't refuse to accept. This unconscionable coalition with money and power is what allowed this dangerous legislation to pass and perpetuates the wholesale legalization of drugs. The prescriptions are then distributed to your Ivy League–graduate doctors who endorse and peddle them to their patients for profit. Trust me, this is no conspiracy theory—this is a conspiracy of absolute truth."

The substantial evidence was proof that my sanity had betrayed me, causing a myriad of delusional, overblown unrealities. I convicted my cognizance of consorting with an ingested foreign terrorist; together they'd petitioned to cause anarchy and conspired to overthrow my sound mental judgment. Those stealthy, subversive bastards dressed up like innocent tablets had embedded a destructive affliction that was bestowed upon my rationalization in hopes of a self-inflicted coup de grace.

I looked down at the prescription bottles that I was holding in the palm of my hand and began gripping them tighter and tighter. Apoplectic with rage, I bum-rushed the kitchen, turned on the faucet, and ripped the tops off the bottles with a single, decapitating blow. I then poured every single pill into the garbage disposal, and listened with contempt to the crushing and grinding destruction of those elusive perpetrators of my delirium.

While I stood guard, assuring the rotary blades continued their obligation to completion, Ronnie interrupted my duties and said, "You're doing the right thing."

Still partially in my stupor, I replied, "Yeah . . . I'm glad it's over." Ronnie reached above the sink and opened up the window shades to reveal a tree that graced my property, and he said, "The battle of the Titans for your sanity isn't over, because you still have that poison running through your veins, and it may take some time before you feel completely whole again. When you feel confused and find yourself in trouble, try to look at the natural surroundings in its purest form. This tree outside your window is only a tree and nothing more, so keep it simple and let this tree be your beacon that symbolizes clarity for what's really real."

I looked at him and said, "Man, you don't understand how far I was about to go . . . just like those pills, I need to get rid of my weapons too."

He looked at me, surprised. "You serious?" I nodded my head to confirm my answer, and he said, "Are you sure that you're coherent enough right now to make the decision in getting rid of your entire mini-arsenal of mass destruction?"

Emphatically, I told him, "Yeah, I know what I'm doing . . . I never want to see them again."

"Wow," he said, "I would've never imagined you would be willing to part with them, but I support you, bro."

"Do you have a guy that I can deal with?" I asked.

He pulled out his phone, scrolled through his contacts and texted me a number. "This is a guy who occasionally does business with some Archangels in my crew; he'll take them off your hands and compensate you well for them."

Receiving the text, I said, "Nikolay?"

"Yeah, he's Russian," Ronnie said. "Give me at least a couple days to contact him and let him know to take care of you."

CHAPTER 16
SABBATICAL CONQUEST

During the course of a semi-lethargic week, I was assigned custodianship to provide laborious maintenance of my saneness for an enduring twenty-four-hour shift per day. Occasionally, I had to get a glimpse of the "reality tree" during my recovery, to reacclimatize with the environment. Once my surroundings appeared firm, I ran a psychological diagnostic check on my faculties, and received a status report that everything was back to normal because I was familiarized with the monotonous, substandard quality of life I knew all too well. My life was dull and disheartening again. I just couldn't understand why every step I took forward ended up being a landmine of melancholy and disaster. Being alive and sad was an exhausting occupation. Living consumed every ounce of optimism with a voracious appetite and left a pile of cynicism that smelled like fecal matter. Jackie once told me that happiness was the treacherous culprit who would betray me someday, and now I knew what he meant; his warning had revealed the hidden truth.

I began to believe that maybe I was cursed, but I wasn't too sure about that impression because I wasn't a superstitious person who believed in bad luck, hexes, and jinxes. I only knew that something beyond my understanding was going on that provoked my ceaseless adversities. I was mentally malnourished, my physicality showing visual signs of fragility, and on top of that, my regular program was interrupted with a severe weather forecast about my future that flashed the message THIS IS NOT A TEST across my teleprompter. My spiritual administration didn't have the necessary logistic essentials to guarantee a successful win in this expensive campaign, and I needed to find a way to promote myself and raise some capital so I could purchase a much-needed ray of sunshine.

Campaigning for an extraordinary development, I reached out for a symbolizing story with trials and tribulations to provide me the encouragement to defeat my antagonist. The first thing that came to my mind was the struggle my ancestors had to endure with admirable strength and determination to achieve their freedom and get us where we are today. Even though I was ill-prepared, I was inspired to do battle because they fought for me to have these privileges, and I felt I now needed to fight to overcome my adversity, which would loudly express my appreciation. I also remembered that somewhere down the line, someone once told me that nothing worth having comes easy.

My formidable pessimistic conscious and I fought to the death like two equally matched pit bulls, and after a few more days of holistically evaluating all my preceding circumstances with 20/20 hindsight, I had a "eureka" moment: my *choices* were the antecedent to all my problems, because there's a reaction to every action. The very basic laws of physics state that all the events in our lives are precipitated by previous events, no matter if the consequences are positive or negative. All I had to do was think of life like I'm playing a strategic game of chess, or better yet, the twenty-five hundred-year-old game invented by the Chinese called Go. Then, make my next move my best move. I was pumped like the head cheerleader at a pep rally and shouted, "Hell, yeah!" Because at that seminal moment, I had it all figured out. With this theoretical science, I would be able to move forward with my life and forecast a brighter future with advantageous results—even the possibility of becoming an esteemed life coach to get a gallant recognition from the mayor, who would be honored to offer me the keys to the city.

Excited, I asked myself, *what's my next move?* With my thinking cap on, I began to think very deliberately, like I'd never thought before, to assert a power play that would catapult me into a remarkable tour de force of sublime success. I thought and thought and thought, then cogitated some more, but the harder I tried, the more my organic ideation degenerated into something that was somewhat synthetically useless. I was disappointed in the deduction, but that was the brutal, honest, filthy truth. The dirty, microscopic residue only left me enough soil to grow a Chia Pet named Misery to comfort me in my lonesomeness. My ingenious maneuvering tactics ended before it started. I was definitively no Bobby Fisher in the sport of strategizing, and it was a no-brainer why I lost a lot at board games. So now, I was back at ground zero with shit on the brain, because all of my wonderful ideas end up getting flushed. Damn, my life sucked!

On a Saturday evening, I had a scheduled meeting with the Russian named Nikolay, to look over my cache of weapons and negotiate a monetary settlement for trade. So I began organizing all my ordnance inside Valhalla on top of my pool table, with crates of various calibers of ammunition adjacently aligned on the floor. Before I could finish, my doorbell rang. I looked at the clock and realized that I was running behind time for our private meet and greet.

I dropped what I was doing and proceeded to the front door to welcome him. He showed up with his hair pulled back into a ponytail, wearing a Rolex timepiece, and dressed with finesse. He was carrying a slender, blue-eyed Siamese cat that he had clothed to look like a professional lady. Nikolay was roughly six feet tall, with a muscular build like a fitness trainer. *His appearance was definitely intuitive with his choice for a domesticated pet*, I thought. But I immediately disliked this guy; his overconfidence in showing up at my house looking like a counterfeit Steven Seagal was repulsive. To be honest, I objected him for the fact that he smelled better than I did. And because he looked at me like I was a discarded booger, picked from the nose of a hobo and flung to the sidewalk. I got past my insecurities, welcomed him inside and led him and his feline companion to inventory the weaponry.

Inside the Hall of Valhalla, I asked him to give me a moment while I finished the assemblage of my firearms. After a couple of minutes, I told him I was prepared. He then gestured with his hand as if he were asking if it was okay to place his kitty-cat on the floor. I confirmed that it was fine. He took his time, examining them meticulously like he was an adept gunsmith.

After he surveyed my catalog of weapons, he picked up his pussy, casually sat down, and began stroking her short coat of fur. I was unsure about what he thought because his demeanor was very cavalier, until he finally spoke in a low baritone pitch with a European accent. "I would like your permission to be blunt, if I may?"

"Yeah, go ahead," I said.

"You don't look so good," he said to me. "Tell me why you don't want your babies anymore—and I say *babies* because they're immaculate. You took good care of them, ergo I know they're special."

I was insulted and said, "Why does it matter? Are we going to do business or what?"

He said, "Sure, we're going to do business. I'm a cosmopolitan professional, and I apologize if I offended you."

I dropped my guard. "It's cool, man, I know I look like stir-fried shit—that's the reason I have a therapist."

"I want your weapons," Nikolay continued, "but I'm a man with many resources, and I have an instinctive sixth sense of clairvoyance that I've acquired since I was a boy in Moscow to see things the average person cannot. Maybe I can offer you more than a single service to benefit you; I'm a diversified gentleman with international capabilities of giving satisfaction."

I was bewildered and then I thought, *oh my goodness, this dude is a pimp and he's trying to peddle me a hooker.* I said, "Look, man, oochiecoochie poontang chow mein is the last thing on my mind right now—thanks, but no thanks."

He laughed and said, "I'm not a pimp, but I am a man of leisure. So, if you could go anyplace in the world, where would it be?"

I thought it was an awkward question, but I still gave it some thought before I said, "I don't know, maybe some desolate place where I could be forgotten about."

He said, "You're not a hard man to please, and forgive me for saying, but you do look like you could use a fresh breath of life to circulate in your lungs. If you can accept my offer for your weapons, I'll throw in an all-expenses-paid vacation to Argentina inside an up-scale five-star hotel for a week. It'll be a morale booster . . . providing you that vital spark you need back into your existence my friend, yes?"

I contemplated the gesture and said, "How much will you give me for everything?"

"Fifty thousand," he said.

I thought about it for a moment and said, "I don't know."

"Okay," he said, "two-week vacation and not another day. This resort is the crème de la crème, people there are wonderful, and the women are exquisite. My friend, a place like this with fifty thousand dollars extra to spend, you will be the Americano Burger King, and have it exactly your way."

"Maybe some other time. I'm not interested in having fun right now. If anything, I need to disappear."

He said, "I make those types of accommodations also, so would you like it to be temporary or permanent?"

I went to the mini-fridge and retrieved myself a beer, mostly to give me time to think. I took my time coming back, still contemplating my not-so-serious request. After painstaking consideration, I looked at him and said, "Indefinite, and I mean untraceable. But I'm not sure about Argentina . . . give me something in Northern Siberia. Maybe I can learn how to build an igloo and practice naked yoga."

He said, "What in the hell are you, the domestic abominable snowman? That place is depressing. People don't go to hell to feel better. Argentina is paradise, the world's best-kept secret—it's my little piece of Arcadia right here on earth, with handsome beaches and very attractive oceans. Myself and Miss Argentina vacation there quite often in our bungalow on the waters."

"Miss Argentina, huh?"

He stroked his companion and said, "Yes, Versailles is my distinguished lady friend right here. I named her after the Château palace in France because of their matching exquisiteness. She has won the supreme title of all cats to be Miss Argentina for the past two consecutive years. The beautiful metropolis of Buenos Aires is where I found her—she's an Argentinian national from a royal bloodline. Genetically for that reason, she has inherited a refined sense of style as you can see. But trust me, you won't regret it. You can live there indefinitely . . . as long as you like."

"How much?" I asked.

"It will cost you an additional ten thousand dollars. It's not cheap to make someone disappear without a trace, and that's much less than the going rate for my diligence with acquiring you a new identity, passport, and documentation making you an Argentine citizen plus flight accommodations."

I confidently said, "Sure, let's do it! But I need this pronto . . . so tell me, how soon can you make me vanish?"

"I can work on it A-S-A-P, and by this time next week, you will be living a subterranean lifestyle indefinitely," he told me.

"Can you guarantee me that no one will know anything about this?" I asked.

"Of course. Work like this I operate confidentially . . . it's always best. The only three on this planet who will know is you, me, and Versailles."

"I can't thank you enough." I said. Then I walked over to my mini-fridge, pulled out another Corona, and offered it to Nikolay so that we could toast to solidify our prearrangement.

He said, "I'm sorry, forgive me, but I don't drink alcoholic beverages. I did notice that you had a bottle of luxurious H20 by Fillico. If I'm not imposing, Versailles and I could salute with that . . . we sort of have an expensive taste."

I thought to myself, *wow, this guy and his lady friend are brazenly chic . . . let me hurry up and get them out of here before he orders some hors d'oeuvres to be delivered first-class via Learjet.* I handed over the Fillico water with a little bit of animosity, because that two-hundred-dollar bottle of liquid, imported from Osaka, Japan, was a memento given to me by Cowboy on one of our investment transactions, which ended up costing me much more than a fine-cut dazzling glass with a golden crown. But I cracked a smile, we held our drinks of choice in the air, and made a salute to our arrangement. Nikolay then told me that he would come back to procure the ordnance and have my legal tender, along with my traveling materials, the following Saturday.

With less than a week to prepare for a journey to kick-start the genesis of my new life, the very first thing I did Monday morning, was drive to the bank and liquidate all the remaining funds from my checking account. Then I purchased a new wardrobe of tropical clothing and anxiously counted down the days to my newfangled adventurous beginning.

All week long, I fantasized about my identity makeover and imagined myself living a bohemian lifestyle at the beachfront. Along with drinking margaritas with the locals, playing volleyball with the unsuspecting tourists in my ultra-tight Speedos, allowing urchin children to bury me in the gritty sand and surf daily with the beach bums. I also entertained the idea of adopting a golden Labrador retriever as a companion so I could throw Frisbees in his mouth like they do in the commercials. Nostalgically, I thought to myself that I couldn't imagine any other place to be freer from the melancholy that inundated my existing life, than this idyllic paradise on earth that seemed so serene.

I woke up on my final day of purgatory and welcomed the morning with a self-prepared breakfast that looked like burnt dog shit. But to me, it tasted like blazed victory, because my luggage was packed with all the personal amenities that I would need for my exodus. I walked around my home to get a final look at everything that I'd acquired over my lifetime; several of the items had a profound sentimental value attached to them, so it was only intuitive to drift into a reminiscent ambiance of belonging. Thinking about delightful moments spent with my family injected a dubious outlook on my endeavors abroad.

Now I wasn't too sure about my pursuit of solitude in this expeditious journey. Contemplating the probability of my choices, I thought, *what if I'm still not happy and I regret it?* Proposing another question, I thought, *what if I absolutely enjoy my new life and become totally unconcerned about my family's well-being?* Observing the emotive possibilities was the antithesis of one another, I wondered, *what type of man would that make me for quitting on my family, by escaping responsibilities to live a subterranean life alone? Staying, would that make me acutely insane for failing to recognize that my overall health was deteriorating for the sake of being optimistic about an irrevocable relationship that's clearly dead?* At that moment, I became very ambivalent and had to take a seat to sort through my emotions. I deconstructed my known quandaries, evaluated the dichotomies with a sagacious perspective of what was best for everyone, and the tallying results were still inconclusive. I reached into my pocket and pulled out a quarter to decide my fate. *Heads* would mean spontaneity, optimistically blow into the wind of anonymity, and explore adventurous opportunities abroad. *Tails* would represent commitment, an ambassador of unconditional hope for a model family, which would obligate me to try again. I flipped the coinage in the air above the dinette table. The coin ascended to its highest point and then descended, landing on the table and danced like a twirling ballerina before it rested on *heads*. I picked it up, inspected it, and noticed a microscopic piece of lint on the opposite side making that side heavier. For that technicality, I sanctioned a do-over. I blew the quarter with a strong pneumatic pressure from my lungs to remove the fiber and flipped it again. The coin went up, came down, and landed flat on *heads* again without bouncing. I've never seen a coin do that on a hard marble surface, and it was discombobulating trying to fathom if that was even possible. I shook off the perplexity of that omen and took matters into my own hands.

I pulled out my phone and contacted Cat. When she answered, I told her that I was going out of town to visit a relative for a couple of weeks. Then I asked her if she could bring the kids by so that I could see them before my trip. She told me that they were out on one of their Candy Crush girls' retreats, but she agreed to bring them by in a couple of hours when they were finished. The timing couldn't have been more perfect to provide me the opportunity for a potential reunification with my family. If all failed, Nikolay was still scheduled to arrive and acquisition his newly acquired weapons, as well as provide me my disappearing supplies.

I grabbed a pen and notebook, entered the Hall of Valhalla to get comfortable before they arrived. Sitting down, I began to write a structured love letter of what I wanted to profess. Because I wanted to ensure that everything I proposed was perfect, since this was my final attempt to reestablish something that had the potential of being a beautiful thing. After I finished my heartfelt declaration, I turned on the television and watched sports to pass the time.

A couple hours later, I heard a car pull up outside the garage door. Assuming it was my family; I ripped the sheet of paper out of the notebook, quickly crammed it inside of my pocket, and opened up the garage door. My daughters' smiles were bigger than Texas when they saw me, and mine was wider than the universe. Cat got out of the car to help them get out, and they all ran and jumped in my arms. Cat stayed by her car and waved hello. I told the kids to go inside the house and wait on me, since I needed a minute to speak to their mother.

I approached Cat and asked, "Would you like to come inside and wait while I spend time with the girls?"

"No thanks," she said, "I'll just wait out here in my car. I hope thirty minutes is enough time for you, because I have to get them home and feed them—we're starving."

I tried to convince her to join us. "You don't want to wait in your car for that long, come on inside . . . at least be courteous enough to allow me to fix you a drink."

She thought about it for a moment and then said, "Sure."

We were walking toward the entrance of the garage when my daughter Bamm-Bamm picked up one of my small-arms weapons and said, "Daddy can I play with this?"

I was stunned that she was holding a real weapon, and I used my authoritative voice, yelling, "Put that fuckin' weapon down, and get your ass in the house with your sisters!"

My aggressive reaction startled Cat, and when she saw the weapon, along with all the others straddled across the pool table, she stopped in her tracks and said, "No, I'm not going in. I'll stay in my car."

As she walked back to her car, I caught up with her and grabbed her arm. "It's okay."

She snatched her arm from me and said, "I don't think so, Michael—I'll just come back and pick them up later."

I touched her arm again and said, "Well, just let me talk to you for a minute."

Pulling her arm from me again, she said, "Don't touch me, and leave me alone!"

She hurriedly pulled out her keys and attempted to get in her car. I was desperate for my last opportunity, so before she could enter her car, I grabbed her, picked her up off the ground, and carried her into Valhalla as she screamed, "Help . . . please, somebody help me!"

I made it to the control box, closed the garage door, and placed her down on the floor. I looked at our children; impending doom was graffitied on their face like a decommissioned subway train in the South Bronx. Cat continued screaming and her body shook violently. With dread in her eyes, she said with a trembling voice, "Please, Michael, let us go!"

The children then ran over and huddled up with their mother and began reiterating her plea: "Daddy, please don't hurt our mommy!"

I was out of breath from the adrenaline of carrying a very pregnant Cat inside Valhalla while she fought me, so I couldn't say anything for a moment. While catching my breath, I wondered why they were reacting so dramatically. I attempted to calm the situation so that I could express why I wanted them there and shouted, "Everyone shut up!" I was able to tone down the pandemonium low enough for them to hear me say, "I have something for you."

I reached in my back pocket, and Cat screamed, "Please don't kill us—we're your family!" The kids' cries were ear-piercing as they continued clinching their mother tightly.

I pulled out my love letter, unfolded it, and said, "Calm the hell down . . . I just want to tell you something I wrote down that's been on my mind." They all stopped screaming, and looked at me awkwardly, as if they just learned they were selected to be contestants for the world's most horrible game show. I said, "What, why y'all looking at me like that? I wasn't going to do anything."

Cat said, "Well, you got all your fucking guns and ammo out on display. I thought you were going to shoot us."

"Oh, that's horrible," I said, now realizing why they'd reacted so strongly. "I'm so sorry. That was a misunderstanding, but let me tell you why you're here." I paused to grab a towel to wipe the sweat from my face and then said, "Since the very first moment I met you—"

"Michael, hold up, I'm having contractions," Cat said, while grabbing her stomach.

"Wow, you sure it's not gas?" I asked.

"Yes, I'm positive it's not that. I've been pregnant three times before this one, so I know what gas feels like."

Not knowing what else to do, I stood there and shrugged my shoulders to denote that I was clueless. Cat said, "Michael, it's way too early for me to have contractions this intense—I'm only five months pregnant—call an ambulance right now!"

I helped her to the sofa while she cringed in excruciating pain. Again she said, "Please call an ambulance before I lose the baby!"

After instructing the kids to go in the house and wait for me inside, I speedily pulled out my phone, dialed 911, and requested emergency care. Cat was moaning in pain and breathing heavily like she was in labor. I felt useless, so I paced around with my hands on the top of my head, wondering what I had done. *What in the hell is going on . . . I can't do anything right . . . all my efforts are sabotaged. Why does everything I do turn into a tragedy?* I thought.

Before I could make sense of it all, I heard the ambulance pull up. As soon as I opened the garage door, the paramedics immediately rushed in carrying a gurney and escorted Cat into the ambulance and secured her inside. Quickly, I went into the living room and told our children to stay inside the house until their grandmother could come over to watch them. Running out the house at breakneck speed, I leaped into the rear of the ambulance, held Cat's hand, and said, "I promise everything will be okay, and I'm going to be here for you the entire time."

While they hastily drove to the nearest hospital, I felt horrible and regretted trying to repair our relationship, because my reconciliation plan was a grand fiasco. Upon arrival, the paramedics placed Cat in a wheelchair, and rushed her into Labor and Delivery with me by her side.

Not long after they placed her on the delivery bed, Cat began to shout that she was in a lot of pain. The doctor came in, inserted his latex-gloved hand into Cat's vaginal cavity and said, "Yep, you're about to have a baby."

"But no, it's too soon!" Cat said, frantic.

The doctor looked at her and said, "I'm sorry." Then he began to triage the nurses accordingly.

Everyone bypassed me while my head bounced around like a pogo-stick in the center of a merry-go-round. I stood there, useless, until a nurse grabbed both of my shoulders and said, "Sir, everything is going to be fine. This happens frequently. But I'm going to need you to have a seat out of the way, okay?"

I complied with her request, found a seat in the corner and watched how organized disorganization looked. The nurses encouraged Cat to push, and suddenly the doctor had a very small preemie in the palm of his hands. They cut the waxy umbilical cord, placed her inside an incubator and instantly rushed the newborn to the Neonatal ICU.

Cat immediately asked, "Is the baby going to survive?"

The staff gave her a discouraging look because the likelihood of a child surviving outside of its mother's womb in the second trimester was highly unlikely. While the doctor removed the placenta, he said, "We're going to try our best." But Cat knew what that meant, and she began to cry. I came to her side, gave her a maudlin hug and held her hand for comfort.

※※※

Inside Cat's recovery room, the doctor returned within an hour. "I'm sorry. We weren't able to save your child."

Cat began to cry again, and the doctor informed her that they were having a difficult time stopping her from bleeding and said, "If we can't control your excessive amount of postpartum blood loss right now, we're going to have to take you into surgery." The doctor then began to probe Cat's uterus to locate and control the hemorrhage.

I transferred my useless hindquarters back into the "nonessential chair" before I got reprimanded again. I continued to observe, hopeful for an expedient resolution, until the doctor told Cat that she was going to need surgery to stop the bleeding and a blood transfusion. The orderlies took control of Cat's gurney and wheeled her into ICU, while a nurse guided me to the waiting area.

I impatiently waited for an update that never came. After a while, I was too afraid to ask, fearing the worst. I finally got the courage to leave my self-appointed seat, marched up to the kiosk desk, and asked the clerk for an update on Cat's status. She confirmed that she was still in surgery, but she wasn't able to provide me with her current condition. I paced for a moment until I couldn't take it anymore and told the clerk that I needed to talk to the doctor. She informed me that he was still in the operating room. Irritated, I said, "Well, you need to get me someone up here who knows what's going on with her condition this very minute, and not someone who has five-minute-old news. I need seconds-to-a-minute update, because this is crucial and my nerves are bad." She displayed an affable understanding and appeased me by picking up the phone and making a call.

The receptionist might as well had sent the message attached to a quadriplegic turtle, because I still waited a nerve-racking extent of time, while invisible bugs crawled underneath my skin forcing me to scratch away. Tardily, Cat's doctor finally agreed to speak to me and requested that I be escorted to the back where he met me in the hallway. "Sir, we stabilized the hemorrhage, but she lost a lot of blood and now she needs a lot of rest."

"Okay," I said, "I want to see her."

He said, "Well, that's another thing; she's in a coma right now because of the significant blood loss."

It felt like King Kong punched me in the solar plexus. "But you said the hemorrhaging was stabilized, so that means you stopped the bleeding, right?"

"Yes, we did stop the bleeding," he said, "but we weren't able to replenish all the blood that she lost because she used all the blood for her type that we had stored."

"This is a hospital—how in the hell do you run out of blood?"

"We *do* have more blood; we just don't have any more of her specific blood type at this time, but please calm down because we have more being delivered."

"How soon?"

"Roughly forty-five minutes to an hour."

"That's too long—she could be dead by then. Use mine."

"Sir, what's your blood type?"

"A-something, I think. What difference does it make, just give her the blood!"

"Sir, it's not that simple," he said. "Even if we verify that you are of the A blood type, she could give you blood, but you would not be able to give blood to her because she is type O. Besides, even if you could, your blood would have to go through a screening process and that takes time. It's just protocol."

I couldn't believe what I was hearing, so I got angry and started pacing again. The doctor approached me and said, "Sir, we are going to do everything possible to give her the best care available . . . we have an excellent team here, and I can assure you that everyone will be giving one-hundred percent. You could come see her if you like."

When he mentioned that I anxiously said, "Yes, I want to see her."

He guided me down the hallway and led me to her recovery room. I paused at the entrance when I saw Cat, because she had equipment all around her: IVs for each arm, a pulse oximeter clamped on her finger, EKG machine with wires to check her heart rate, and an apparatus covering her mouth and nose to help with breathing. A single nurse appeared busy, as she moved around tinkering with some of the devices to monitor Cat's on-going progress. I moved my legs, took the first step that nearly felt like I had a million more to go, until I eventually stood by her side and looked at her almost lifeless body, now at the mercy of the machines and the care of the staff. I felt weak and sick inside, nauseated, and I soon became light-headed. The doctor approached me and asked me if I would like time alone with her.

"Yes, thanks," I said.

He asked the nurse to step out for a moment, and before he exited the room I said, "Doctor, I need to ask you something." He stood by the door, and I asked, "What are her chances?"

He closed the door and walked over to me. "Fifty percent, once we can get started on the blood transfusion again. The saline helps keep the circulatory system open and keeps her hydrated, but getting more whole blood in her is vital."

I shook my head. "So that means her chance for survival right now is even lower than that, huh?"

"Unfortunately, yes," he answered.

The hair on the back of my neck and arms rose up, giving me the chills with goose bumps; I started rubbing myself for comfort. The doctor excused himself, telling me that he was going to give me some privacy. I pulled out my crumpled declaration, unfurled it, and began reciting my affection word-for-word.

"Since the very first moment I met you, I was enchanted by your beauty and mesmerized by your charm. I said to myself, if I could have a woman like that, I would be very fortunate, and I'd go through hell to keep her. These last few months without you have felt like hell on earth. If there is such a thing as a bottomless pit with fire and brimstone and grotesque entities awaiting me, I'd trek through it barefoot, soaked in gasoline, and with an S on my chest, because you are my Lois Lane. We've built a gorgeous family, with the most energetic, phenomenal children . . . but I have to admit that they can be extremely obnoxious and mischievous at times. I'm sure the triple-threat twerk team will strike again, and I'll be there to catch them . . . and when I do, I just might join in because I miss us so much. With you—it's the trivial things that I miss the most, like how the water drips down your face after you just washed your hair, or how, after we've spent the entire day together, you turn to me and say hello as though you've been missing me all day. I would do anything to get us back to that place, when we were at the happiest point of our life together. I'd seize that moment and place it into a shatterproof snow globe to withstand everlasting eternity. Because I understand now, what we once had was delicate . . . and should be protected and preserved like a priceless, cherished antiquity. So if this dream is a realism that you would still like to possibly capture, let me know what needs to be done."

I placed the letter back into my pocket, looked at her motionless body, and commenced to adlib. "That is what I wanted to say to you back at the house before my proposal went bottoms-up. Now, because of me, you're not able to answer, and I'm not sure if you ever will. It's my fault; every imaginable thing that's wrong right now is my doing. I just don't understand why this never-ending series of unfortunate events are following me. Something far beyond my understanding is going on, but whatever it is, it's definitely no friend of mine. Regardless, I'm going to stay with you as long as it takes for you to get better, even if you can't hear me. Just hold on—please don't die."

Despite the effusive adrenaline rushing through my veins about Cat's dire circumstances, I carefully chose my next words to accurately depict my devotion. "What I'm about to say is no metaphor . . . if my life could be taken to spare yours, I would die for you a thousand times. I would sit crisscross applesauce, cross my heart and hope to die a horrible death before I allow you to leave me. If it's true that I have a soul, may it be eternally cursed if I ever break this oath."

I then pulled the ring out of my pocket and reached over, placing it on her finger. Holding her hand, I said, "If you could forgive me again and do me the honor of becoming my wife like once upon a time we spoke of, I promise . . . I'll provide a kingdom in my heart that will spread wider than the Persian Empire and build a palace of love more grandeur than the Taj Mahal." I looked at her more closely and noticed a tear falling from the edge of her eye. I leaned over and placed a tender kiss upon her cheek.

I left the room desperately in need of a four-leaf clover, a lucky rabbit's foot, and a couple Hail Mary's to get our family through this abysmal succession of endless tragedies. After exiting the hospital, I fancifully looked up and wished upon a star that Home Depot sold a crises button that I could press to automatically rejuvenate my life with a desired makeover.

Shortly after my juvenile wishful thinking, I flagged down a taxicab to take me home so that I could get some clothes for an overnight stay at the hospital. During the commute I checked my phone and noticed that I had several missed calls from Nikolay; I neglected to contact him back, because our arrangement was immaterial and obsolescent at that moment.

I entered my home and encountered my mother and children with trepidation written all over their faces. My mother reluctantly asked me, "How is she?"

I hesitated and grit my teeth, shaking my head from side to side. "Not good, and she wouldn't be there if it wasn't for me, Ma. She might not make it! I just came back to get some clothes. I'm going back up to the hospital, so take the kids home with you for the time being, please."

The kids got emotionally agitated, and started asking me question all at once. But, their inquiries together sounded like Charlie Brown's anonymous schoolteacher from the cartoon *Peanuts*. "Wahhh, wah, wah, wah, wahhh. Wah, wahhh, wha, wha, wha, whahhh."

My mother intervened, and attempted to answer their questions one-by-one. So, I excused myself and entered my bedroom, closed the door, and quickly packed an overnight bag. I came out of the room and saw that my mother and children hadn't left yet. I was too distraught for any farewells, so I swung my bag across my shoulder and headed for the front door.

My mother caught up with me, grabbed my hand before I could make it out of the door, and said, "Son, I know what you're going through, and I understand how you feel. God is always in control, and you need to know that regardless of what happens, everything will be fine, so don't be too hard on yourself because everything happens for a reason."

That statement hit me like a ton of bricks. I dropped my bag and turned around to face her. "So, what are you saying? What exactly does that mean?"

She hesitated and said, "Well, first close the door and come back inside." I closed the door and we walked back into the living room. "I just want to prepare you to accept whatever destiny God has chosen," my mother said. "I'm going to pray very hard for her, and leave it in his hands."

Irritated, I said, "So you're telling me that everything that's going on is happening for a reason only God knows, and he's also the one who ultimately going to make the decision if Cat lives or die?"

"Maybe you're being tested," she said. "I know it's hard to understand and difficult to accept, but God knows what he's doing."

I said, "Hold up, back up . . . what are you talking about, I'm being tested?"

"Do you remember that biblical story about Job, the way he was tested? Maybe God is trying to tell you something."

"Don't compare me to that guy!" I said.

"Michael," she continued, "I wish I could. Job was a loyal, God-fearing, honorable man. He kept the faith through all his trials and tribulations, and that's why God rewarded him seven times more than what was taken from him. Let God in, son; only he can help you."

I got angry and said, "I don't want more! I need what I had! That's what you call help—God allowing his most devoted human to suffer horrendously for the sake of proving to Satan that he would remain loyal? God is omniscient, right? That means he knew what the devil was going to do. He endorsed Satan murdering the man's children, so that makes him an accomplice in my book!"

While my mother stood there quietly, I thought about what I'd just said and glanced at my children, sitting on the couch frightened out of their minds. I said, "Ma, if what you're saying is true, and something morbid happens to anyone in my family for a test or to teach me a lesson, I promise you no one would be safe, and I mean *no one!*"

My kids started crying and my mother consoled them with hugs. Aajani said, "Grandma, I'm scared!"

I didn't want my kids to be afraid so I said, "Ma, can you please leave and take the kids with you?" She approached me and said, "I don't want to leave you, Son."

"Ma, it hurts . . . you don't know the entirety of all the things I've been going through, but I can tell you it's been excruciating and unbearable for too long, and I can't take it anymore. It hurts too bad—I need you to leave."

She couldn't hold back her hidden waterworks any longer and put her hands up to her face and started weeping. I approached her, gently removed her hands from her face, and wiped her tears away with my fingers. "Please, Ma, don't cry."

She held her head down, her tear ducts still overflowing, and she said, "I can't stop crying. I don't want you to hurt yourself, Michael. I don't know what I would do if I lost you."

I asked her to look into my eyes. "I promise you I won't hurt myself."

"Well, please don't hurt anyone else."

"I'm not going to hurt anyone else either," I told her.

"Promise to me again."

I grabbed her hand and said, "You have my word. I promise."

"Okay, so what are you going to do?"

"Something I probably should've done a long time ago."

"I don't like how that sounds."

I paused for a moment and said, "I need to be alone for this."

She said, "I know that you don't want to hear this. But, whatever it is you're talking about doing, I'm going to pray for God to guide your intentions, and I'm going to pray like I've never prayed before for God to deliver you from your pain."

"Okay," I told my mother. But to myself I thought, *you don't understand that what I'm about to do would be considered the ultimate sacrilege, and most certainly unforgivable.*

My mother gathered up the children and abandoned me like I requested, so that I could proceed with my precarious undertakings.

CHAPTER 17
UNSPEAKABLE

Finally, alone, I stood in the middle of my living room and embodied the spirit of a kamikaze warrior, looked up, and impiously addressed God. "You did this to me, didn't you?" I paused for a moment to anticipate God's response and then yelled, "You think this is fuckin' funny? Answer me, goddamnit!"

I took another recess, just in case there was some kind of delayed reaction in the distant line of communication. After what I thought was more than a sufficient amount of time, I disputatiously asked, "Do you think I fear you? Well, I'm not afraid of you. You're the puppet master who's been causing all this mayhem around me and sabotaging all my ambitions since the very beginning. You act like you're running a fuckin' casino up there, gambling with my life as if I can afford to take a loss. Who in the hell do you think you are to play with my life like this? Huh? Who in the fuck do you think you are? I'll tell you . . . you're the master of deception and an insecure bully with a known history of violence; who's a malevolent fearmongerer who operates a faceless barbarity with an infinite amount of mass hysteria and destruction. That's right, I said it! And just in case you didn't know, my inferno of hatred for you has been incubating for a very long time, so you don't want to miss this, because I have a lot more to tell you. You have a severe disconnection with your most intellectual creation, and you're the ultimate oppressor of every living species but yourself, because you're an unsympathetic megalomaniac totalitarian whose entire reign has been scandalous. I bet you look like the lonely prima donna drag queen that had to go to the prom all by her lonesome, because you were too ugly to get a date. You're like an infant who throws temper tantrums when no one wants to play with you, and you offer asylum to submissive people who kiss your ass. It doesn't surprise me why you behave the way you do, and it's obvious why. You didn't have parents to raise you any better, so do you know what that makes you . . . a fucking bastard! That's right, you're the original bastard! You were an accident, so how in the fuck did you get to be in your position to rule? You don't have gladiators either; you got a despicable army of weaklings who are too afraid to stand up against your brutality. I'm not like your beloved Job—he's fuckin' pathetic! That punk don't have a backbone. He tolerated your uncompassionate involvement in condoning the massacre of his innocent children, and that sorry son of a bitch had the audacity to forgive you because in exchange for his loyalty, he was rewarded with more than he ever had. You really believe replacing this man's children with a new family and a greater wealth healed his pain? Job is a lowlife traitor of morality and justice to silence his tongue about your horrific betrayal, in exchange for a golden ticket into your precious heaven of milk and honey. He should be shot on sight! If I ever see him, I'll give him a coward's death. I'm sick and tired of your charades and people's rhetoric about how good you are. Come on, Boogie Man, show yourself. I want to see the *real* face of evil."

I stood there, huffing and puffing, and waited on God to defend himself, to no avail. "Oh, that's right, you'd rather operate with anonymity, right? Well, match your best against me—I'll chastise them all. You have a heaven full of gutless followers with the hearts of cowards anyway. You're a reckless, egotistical dictator that runs a concentration camp of demoralized, emasculated groupies who think you're omnibenevolent, and they're pathetically blind to the fact that you're really their oppressor. You don't have me fooled, because I know your modus operandi. I don't want your dystopian dreamland. Fuck you! I'm going to martyr myself and go on a crusade to become a vigilante and get some restitution for everyone you have abused. You're the enemy of the entire universe and definitely not worthy to be called the king of kings, the lord of lords, or even a God . . . so if you don't like it, come and do something about it, tough guy."

I got in a fighting stance in the likeness of a silverback gorilla and told him, "Come fight me—give me all you got and annihilate me right now. What the fuck you waiting on? Hurry up and destroy me!" I stood my ground and began swinging my fists, bobbing and weaving until I realized I was tiring myself out by fighting an opponent that wasn't there.

I immobilized my unsuccessful fight and placed my hands on my knees with the fatigue of a golden-glove champion pugilist. "So you don't want to fight me . . . you probably couldn't make it because you're too busy fuckin' up someone else's life." I took my hands off my knees and pointed up to the heavens. "If this is one of your perverted tests, and you harm anyone in my family, I'll—" I didn't complete my ventilation because I couldn't think of anything that I could practically do to ultimately protect them or how to strike back with vengeance at something I couldn't see. I paced while clutching my fists, bit and grinded my teeth, and thought extremely hard about how to make a calculated, preemptive attack.

I stopped dead in my tracks, looked above me and said, "You want to see some real courage? I'll show you a brave heart." I went into the Hall of Valhalla and grabbed some black spray paint, a knife, candles, and a lighter. I carried my items back into the living room, lit the candles, drew *666* on the wall, and spray-painted a pentagram on the carpet.

Turning off the lights to accentuate the caliginous mood, I placed myself in the epicenter of the painted diabolical representation of evil. Because my intention was to demand a phenomenon from the archenemy of God with so much desire and intensity that the force of the universe would stand still and pay attention.

"Satan! I know you can hear me. I have a request, so I need you right now. I'm sure you know that God is the supreme undesirable, and it's no secret that I reject and rebuke him. He's the personification of a bipolar, self-serving narcissistic creep who I intimately denounce. You're the divinely supreme almighty God of the dark side, who has remained consistent with your undeviating malignant intentions. If you could bless me by granting the request I'm about to make, my soul will worship you with the utmost commitment and strength. I'll demonstrate to you an extraordinary determination that will make anyone who serves underneath you envious about this sincere pledge that I'm about to make. I promise you that no one before me or after me will be as honored and elated to stand tall and profess his allegiance, loyalty, and devotion."

I glanced over at a family portrait that hung above the mantel on the fireplace, and tears began to cascade down my cheeks like Niagara Falls. That pictorial, capturing a loving moment, invigorated my purpose even more. "Happiness is what I want." Then I pointed at the picture and said, "Those are the smiling faces that could fill my emptiness with joy. That beautiful lady right there is in the hospital dying in a coma right now, and she is an integral piece to this story. I need her desperately!"

I took a short intermission to catch my breath. My body language had been so energized with my convictions that perspiration began to soak through my clothes.

Tightening my fists, I then flexed my muscles, and said, "Lucifer, if you can grant me back my family in whole with happiness we've never experienced before . . . I'll be so honored that my soul will shake violently with acceptance to celebrate this as the best offering you've ever had. Also, for this contract to be valid, and yourself awarded such a warrior, you have to provide me my mortal salvation until the seventeenth of October, on my one-hundredth birthday. But you need to know that I will not worship you in this life form, and I am only acknowledging you right now at this time for this arrangement only. My home will be my temple, my family will be my religion, and on that lovely, dreadful day, I will fulfill my end of this agreement and hit the ground running, surpassing anything horrific before me. I'll take pleasure in becoming the ultimate apex predator and put the dark into darkness. I promise to quarterback your legion of demons and become the *worst* terrorist anyone has ever seen. The world is going to be horrendous, because it's going to be a bloodbath. Those are my terms . . . so if you want me, I'm right here."

I unbuttoned my shirt and took it off, tossing it to the side. I picked up my knife and slid the blade across the palm of my left hand, slicing a superficial cut through my flesh, and pitched it to the side also. Using the index finger of my right hand like a paintbrush, I dipped into the small puddle of blood and sketched a bull's-eye on my bare chest.

"Come on, you can't miss . . . this is my blood sacrifice." I was amped up like an American muscle car with a full tank of high-octane gasoline at the starting line, waited for my sign of approval to accelerate with explosive speed when suddenly; my phone vibrated and rang as if I were hosting a telethon.

"Wow," I said, "you doing it like that?" I enthusiastically reached in my pocket and pulled out my phone. It was my mom. I turned the lights on as I answered and said, "Ma, I'm in the middle of something right now that's very important. What do you need?"

"Well, I was just checking on you . . . making sure you're okay."

"I'm fine," I said, "but I need to go because I'm doing something special that's about to make a big difference in my life."

Excited, she said, "Thank you, Jesus . . . you're praying to God, aren't you?"

The audacious question instantly made me apoplectic. "Why in the hell would I be praying to an invisible SKY DADDY who doesn't do a damn thing?"

"I'm sorry, son . . . when you mentioned that you were doing something special that's going to make your life better, I just assumed you were referring to praying to the Lord Almighty."

"Almighty—is that what you think about him? Psst, I acknowledge a bigger God. I'm talking about the one with action!"

"I'm confused," she said. "What God are you speaking of that's higher than the almighty God you were raised to believe?"

I said, "Ain't nothing mighty about that nonentity . . . I'm talking about Satan!"

"Huh? What are you saying?"

"You heard me right: Satan is the truth!"

"That's nonsense—you don't know what you mean. Please, son, don't hurt me like this. Never say that again."

"I'm sorry, Mother, it's already done, and I can't take it back. I've just put a smile on the devil's face."

"What are you talking about? What did you do?"

"The unspeakable. It's no secret . . . don't make me say it."

"Please, no you didn't—the devil is a lie!" she implored. "You're just not in your right mind right now, so you don't know what you're talking about!"

Emphatically, I said, "I was fully coherent when I gave my soul to Satan, and I needed it, I wanted it . . . I did it with so much passion that he has to accept me. I'm a fallen angel now because your God didn't want me. Hail Satan!"

My mother burst out crying and started speaking unintelligible gibberish. I lowered the phone and dislodged the battery from the rear compartment and tossed them both to the other side of the room so that I wouldn't receive any more interruptions during my ceremonial offering.

I turned off the lights and stood in the middle of the pentagram and said, "No more playing around . . . give me some hope that's real."

I closed my eyes tightly to commit to an intense level of concentration for a séance with the gatekeeper of darkness. After a moment of meditating, my eyeballs seemed to withdraw so deep into my eye sockets that I felt an aching sensation as though my orbs were about to vanish into the abyss of the Bermuda Triangle like the mysterious disappearance of the USS Cyclops. Gradually, I heard something rattling above my head. I looked up but couldn't make out the source of the suspicious noise. After a short time, the bulbs on the inoperable chandelier began to radiate an ominous, dim glow while it vibrated. I smiled because I knew my master had authorized the opening to the gates of hell. All of a sudden, the dim lights, which were only forty watts, emitted an eye-piercing luminous discharge. The invading light cut through my retina like a Somali pirate assaulting me with a razor-sharp dagger and instantaneously delivered an excruciating pain to my optical nerves. I attempted to open my eyes to see the Prince of Darkness, but the agony of my injurious sight wouldn't allow me the luxury. The pain was unrelenting, so I pronounced my discomfort like a stereotypical damsel in distress and screamed as loud as I could while my defenseless vision was hijacked and taken hostage. Contented with the indicative sign of an unambiguous, hellish presence and desperate to end the agony to my eyeballs, I ransomed my comfort back when I said, "Okay, I'm convinced!"

All at once, every single light bulb in the chandelier exploded into tiny pieces. Shards of thin glass shattered around the room and pelted me as they rained down like little indiscriminate paratroopers. I opened my eyes, and slowly my blurred vision adjusted to the flickering candles and the blackness that served as a gloomy backdrop. I laughed hysterically because I was over-exuberant to succeed in conjuring the greatest all-powerful incorporeal entity that ever existed, not to mention the extent of pride I felt in my fearless audacity to engage in an evil, tabooed destiny that frightened so many. It was ecstatical, and a glorious privilege to open myself up freely in welcoming in the most supreme maleficent entity. After being convinced without any modicum of doubt that my offering was graciously accepted, I prepared for my inductional ceremony by laying my corporeal flesh on top of my constructed sancta to martyrdom my soul for the glory of a worthy cause. Closing my eyes, I spread my arms adjacent to my supine torso and crossed my legs to prepare for my coronation.

"Show me!" I said.

CHAPTER 18

SACRAMENT

I was extremely optimistic and waited for a signage to manifest. When nothing immediately happened, I thought maybe I was too excited, so I started breathing slowly to lower my heartbeat to a more sustainable tempo and attempted to clear my consciousness for a deeper meditative state. With my body relaxed and my entire quintessence free of any restrictions, my thoughts began to travel indiscriminately.

I was lackadaisical about my random contemplations until I noticed there was actually a pattern. My thinking had a systematic direction and theme with all my misdeeds being accessible, even the ones I'd forgotten, starting with the most recent to the most distant in chronological order. I began to feel uncomfortable about the nature of my recollections, because they were shameful. Therefore, I attempted to redirect my thoughts to memories that were nobler, but I was powerless in my attempts to control these unwanted recalls. Then agitation joined the league of botheration, when I was swarmed with images from a slide projector that kept coming, fast and faster in rapid succession, right after another. Feeling sick, repulsion beset upon me until I shouted, "Stop!"

It ceased on my demand, and with warp speed, I was back to the present time. If I'd known it was that easy to end the tour, I would have ended it before it begun, because it was mortifying. After opening my eyes, I sat up and held myself for a moment since I felt an unbelievable surge of empathy for my transgressions. Still embracing myself with a mystified curiosity about the astral projection, I tried comprehending the significance of the transcendental experience.

Not understanding the implication of the ordeal, I wrote it off, laid back down, and closed my eyes again. I then spread my arms and crossed my legs precisely how I was positioned before that bizarre encounter. Starting the process over, I applied breath control and a mental clearance technique to relax myself.

Tranquil from meditating, moments later I received an unspoken invitation of enlightenment. However, I wasn't able to begin my inception without total submission. Without any foreknowledge of potential dangers about this quest, I was very skeptical. This pursuit was peculiar and creepier than anything I'd ever experienced before in my life, so I knew I had to compromise with myself about this journey as if my life depended on it. I was apprehensive about letting myself go because I thought, *what if I acknowledge something that's so mind-boggling and unimaginably freaky that it disrupts my balance, threatens everything I've known as a tangible source of reality, and hurls me into a state of lunacy?* But I was equally optimistic, thinking, *what if I acquire all the hidden answers and knowledge about the entire universe, which will give me an immortal intellectual understanding and the hybrid power of a demigod?*

I weighed my options for a moment and concluded my decision, with self-reflecting rationalization, that this phenomenon was the once-in-a-lifetime opportunity I'd been longing for my whole life, and that I may never get this chance again.

With total submission, I courageously whispered, "Yes." All of a sudden, my gameness hit the gas and transcended me into obscurity. During the commencement of my exploration, I could feel the sensation of still being attached to my body on the floor; it was the cognizance of my very existence that explored these territories weightlessly.

I began to envisage the anonymous future with vivid clarity, starting with our present-day milieu and casually moving forward like a virtual-reality tourist into events that hadn't happened yet. The illustrious father of science fiction, H.G. Wells would've envied my visualization. I thought, *wow, this is fuckin' amazing. I'm experiencing things before they happen.* Some monumental things were shown to me that would be a turning point to revolutionize and shape the course of our future. Also, during my navigation of the premature events, I subjectively thought, *that's easy . . . I could've predicted that outcome without a genie.* I continued my conveyance freely, without dissension, when I was astounded by the concordant magnificence of humankind interacting together holistically for the greater good of everyone.

Evolutionary social progress had evolved into a global equanimity among the communities; hardship and suffering were absent worldwide. There was a wonderful, homogeneous unit of cohesion and equality that was extended to everyone, with the appearance of "all for one and one for all" as the ultimate agenda. We had conquered the idyllic environment with a luxuriant amount of conveniences to ease our way of life. Pleasantries was the universal language, and everyone's personal motivation was constructively eclectic for the benefit of everyone. Growth and development in the field of technological advancement was prevalent everywhere. There was an indisputable consensus that aggressive science held the key to humanity's infinite survival.

With amazing satisfaction, I continued moving onward to the emergence of the inevitable humanistic quality of insatiability, and I became disconcerted because I could prognosticate that things would become dreadful. My attitude was confirmed when

I witnessed how we voraciously challenged ourselves to pursue perfection irresponsibly—efficiency became the most important value, and populations worldwide approved inhumane methods of achieving this objective. I couldn't grasp why people were so dutiful in attaining something egregious without rebellion. It was as if they were automatously obedient.

I tried alerting them, and hollered, "Hey, what are you doing? Don't do that! You're going to hurt us! Stop it!" But my pleas fell on deaf ears because I didn't physically exist in that time period. My presence was in an adjacent parallel dimension that was invisible to them. Ultimately, as their self-destructive pursuits perennially escalated to the point of no return, it happened. The end was absolutely mind-blowing. I was so disturbed by what I'd seen that I catapulted back to the now, jumped up from the floor, hightailed to the kitchen, and threw up in the sink.

CHAPTER 19
EPIPHANOUS

After expelling most of the putrefied content inside my viscus, I flipped on the light switch above the sink and said, "What the hell was that?" I remained in the kitchen hovering over my vomitus until my breathing and heart rate were under control and then tracked back into the living room, devastated over the prophecy. I paced, trying to comprehend what-in-the-world had just happened, and wondered, *why was I shown in great meticulous depth my abject past and the future of doom in grave detail?* For a moment, I couldn't grasp the meaning, nor could I understand what to do with the information, but after a short amount of time, I had a eureka moment for the opportunity of a lifetime.

Extremely happy, I shouted, "This is brilliant! I can write a book about these future events. Dude, you're about to be rich!"

I gloated and grinned like a Cheshire cat while I envisaged riches beyond my wildest dreams that would provide me the similar lifestyle of the rich and famous. Thrilled with how I could be so lucky, I laughed aloud with a superabundance of enthusiasm and jumped up and down, fist pumping. Visually, I fulfilled every desired fantasy of material luxury for my family that wealth could buy. I even regaled the idea of us living an extravagant lifestyle of snobbish socialites with new money for shits-and-giggles. Ridiculously, strolling down my drive-way wearing a bathrobe, loafers, and an ascot choking my neck, just to pick up the morning newspaper in an oversophisticated attempt at trying to impress our affluent neighbors.

After building castles in the air, I went inside my daughter's room, grabbed one of her scholastic notebooks and a pen, and began to notate my calligraphical interpretation of the divination I received for a narrative reference. Subsequently, I began to wonder why I was so lucky; I'm not that smart. Then I thought, *wait, I feel very intelligent . . . my mental faculties are very sharp right now.*

Flipping to an empty page inside the notebook, I challenged myself to do advanced arithmetic. After writing down a complicated algebraic equation, and quickly jotted down the answer, I retrieved a calculator to check my work; to my surprise, it was right. I did it again, and it was correct. Then I moved to calculus, geometry, and trigonometry. I was flabbergasted over my ability to solve these mathematical computations without difficulty.

This was impossible; my acute memory recall and intellect were absolutely remarkable. I knew something miraculous had just happened to give me this extraordinary aptitude, and I was determined to find out what was going on, because I felt like it was handed to me on a silver platter. My brain was scrambled and perplexed about where to even start. I calmed myself down by sitting on the couch, and decided to go over the details of my last twenty-four hours in chronological order up to this point.

I meticulously backtracked my steps down to the finest details like a seasoned criminologist working a high-profile case with an enormous amount of forensics to sift through. My mind was doing recollection somersaults like Dominique Dawes when all of a sudden, it hit me: I made a deal with Satan. I quickly arose from the sofa, stunned with my mouth open, and remained speechless for a moment. Finally, I said, "Wow, all I wanted was my family healthy and back together with smiles, and I get all of this." Acutely confused, but then I thought something supernatural had to have happened for me to receive this type of sentience as a gift. Then, I felt a rumble underneath my feet. Because metaphorically, my stomach fell through my asshole and shook the foundation I stood on.

"No! What the fuck have I just done?" I took a long pause until the consequences of my actions impaled my consciousness. "Fuck . . . Satan is real!" I began to quiver uncontrollably because I knew right then that if Satan was real, so was God.

With my eyeballs big as a Ferris wheel I yelled, "Please take it back—I don't want it!" I hopelessly shook my head in despair because I knew what I'd done was irreversible and my kismet was permanently sealed. For a long while, I just stood there with my head hung low, staring at the floor. I despondently accepted my fate of the damned, for I was certain that my membership was now actively bona fide.

Curiously, I began wondering if other recruits had succeeded in such a way by making a sacrifice to Satan. I asked myself, *is this how people of wealth and power from around the world have gained their success—they willingly traded their eternal souls?* I thought for a moment to answer my own question. *Hmm, I guess the wealthy is a private network of Satan's compatriots, an elite group of selectees, of which I myself am now a member.* I also pondered, *so, does this means that the delegation is aware of me, and what I've just done?* I envisioned the New World Order grinning, welcoming me with open arms, and inducting me into their exclusive brotherhood of corruption. The Illuminati, an axis of evil, who have been shamelessly shaping a fashionable society with excessive greediness and have the sophistication to operate within plain sight of nonmembers. Furthermore, they own an unlimited amount of concerted resources to manipulate governments and control the media with the united goal of pleasing their master.

Right at that moment, I knew that I didn't want to be associated with any consortium of deviltry, and I declared that the *love* of money was the root of all evil. I rushed over to the table, picked up the notebook, and began ripping pages out of the tablet as fast as I could. While I held onto the shredded remains of my futuristic business plan, I screamed as loud as my voice would allow me, "No, I don't want to be a part of this!" Then I tossed the outline across the floor. Extremely remorseful, I fell to my knees and started crying, and humbly stated, "God, I'm sorry; would you please forgive me?"

Instantaneously, without expecting any sort of acknowledgement or leniency, an authoritative, divine feeling seemed to originate from my center and permeate every cell of my body; it was the most illuminating sensation I'd ever felt in my life. Unafraid, I rose to my feet, physically weightless in an erect and dignified comportment to show reverence to this innocuous foreign entity. At that moment, there was an interim period that I witnessed with silent acknowledgement before progressing with a kinetic conversion that began with a valediction of my hostility, resentment, and antipathy. Then there was a singular aura with a magnificent cosmic big bang that brilliantly emanated an ultra-powerful source of spellbinding passion within me. The feeling was so excessively intense that it bestowed a messiah complex upon my self-awareness.

Fretful and confused, I looked down at my exoskeleton. "What am I, Jesus?" The thought of me being the Son of God and exhibiting the physical manifestation of the second coming of Jesus Christ was phenomenally frightening. I started shaking as if I was having an epileptic seizure and said, "No, God, please don't do this to me. I can't handle this burden. Besides, I messed up my body and got too many tattoos . . . I look like a felonious amigo!"

I hyperventilated until I got lightheaded. Right before I lost consciousness, my metacognitive realization kicked in and said, *no, idiot, you're simply having a very profound experience that's awakening your consciousness to an amazing spiritual manifestation of God.*

After a few moments, I regained my strength of cognitive responsiveness. I was suddenly in awe and rapturously elated to be given the honor of experiencing the essence of the Creator. I anxiously went to the Victorian mirror, believing I would see God in the flesh, but the only being I recognized was my own likeness. I perused the familiar reflective image while I moved my limbs around to detect the slightest dissonance between what I was doing compared to what I was seeing, but I distinguished no dissimilarities. Studiously determined to rationalize a transparent answer to this enigma, I took a syllogistical approach to understand my experience, and philosophically concluded that God and I stood homogeneously as one.

CHAPTER 20
CATHARSIS

I was overjoyed with adulation to have the existence of God immanently reside within me, and now that I had God's attention, I looked at myself and asked God, "Why would you forgive me?"

God answered me, devoid of any spoken word. "Because you willed it."

"Okay," I said, "I'm just going to jump right into it and be blunt with you . . . why do you allow people to commit horrible crimes against each other?"

God answered, "The ones who cause suffering with their actions to others are also capable of preventing suffering with an equal benevolent action; every willing person has the freedom of choice."

"Why give us the independence to choose bad choices? Why not restrict us with several options of good choices so that we don't fail?" I asked.

"Because you wouldn't have free will."

I further asked, "How are our choices considered to be free will, when you already know what we're going to do?"

"My intelligence of your destiny doesn't coerce any decisions that were influenced by your desire," God responded.

"Why don't you get involved to help people that are in need?"

"I do," God answered. "I inspire everyone, too."

"What does that mean?" I said.

"The intuitive compassion you feel to change things and help someone in need is the stimulus that I naturally provide to make a difference."

"Why do you permit calamitous natural disasters to happen?" I queried.

"All that's unambiguous or supernatural to you is codependent on a vibrant duality, which constitutes the essential ontological development of all things in existence and their kinetic perpetuity to exist."

"Oh, I get it," I said. "To achieve sustainability, nature's indiscriminate wrath is an inevitable natural reaction in our biodiverse, self-governing ecosystem. Everything in an environment has an equivalent, dynamic counter-dualism for a ubiquitous equilibrium."

"That's true."

"Hmm," I said. "Like infinite has finite; strong has weak; light has dark; water has fire; up has down; right has left; in has out; back has forth; future has past; happy has sad; smart has dumb; rich has poor; nice has mean; big has small; male has female; belief has disbelief; beauty has ugly; yes has no; love has hate; winner has loser; life has death, and good has evil."

I then stopped and realized the gravity of what I'd just said. My vertical posture slumped over like a curvature question mark; I was dumbstruck over the realization of this datum. At a loss for words with a mild degree of confusion, I struggled to open my cottonmouth and had just enough moisture for my vocal cords to stutter. "You . . . you created evil . . . but, but I don't understand . . . why would you do that to us?" With the temperament of an inquisitive scholastic pupil, I expected the quiddity to my enigmatic question to be complicated.

The answer was simpler than I expected. "I've allowed the potential of evil to coexist and challenge the moral fragility of the free-thinking kind to become empowered with a collective aptitude for compassion to unanimously recreate a peaceable society."

I then asked, "Are we running afoul from exploiting our resources?"

"Every quantity of resource has its own unique significant value and is finitely available for authentic reproduction or artificial production. There's a great detriment to overexploitation that could threaten the availability of all resources. Frugality, together with efficiency, is an effective solution to extend a sustainable existence.

"Are our tenacious scientific exploratory endeavors to travel and understand the cosmos and everything within it a transgression against you?"

"Not at all. The irresistible obsession of gaining knowledge is a quality I encourage for sustainability and intellectual advancement."

I thought about the lucid prophetical revelation I'd had, and with a dejected bearing, I spoke to God and proposed my hypothesis. "That futuristic vision I received about our destiny is true . . . we're not going to survive . . . that's exactly how we're going to meet our demise, right?"

"It doesn't have to be."

I exhaled with relief, knowing that our civilization still had a choice in our destiny. I was running out of questions and wasn't sure how long I was going to have this exclusive opportunity. I thought about what would be the question of all questions, and after a brief moment, I asked, "Why? What's the meaning of all of this, and what is the objective?"

God gave a simplistic, unfulfilling answer. "It will be revealed in time."

I was slightly disappointed not to have the question satisfied, but to compensate for that omission I figured it was probably best to be intrigued about the quality of not knowing.

Then, overflowing with guilty unhappiness, I realized and acknowledged that I would have to praise God. I took a deep breath and courageously exhaled my hesitation, and I said, "Hold up. I'm not going to worship you. It's too much—I just can't do it. Taking care of my family and instinctively following my heart with what is right is enough religion for me."

I stood there fidgeting, waiting for a slap to kingdom come, but God answered, "When you truly love others like you adore yourself . . . you are worshiping Me."

Suddenly, I was taken back a bit and stunned into silence, because I was generationally taught to believe my whole life that monetary offerings and a tedious routine of worship was at the core of having a close relationship with God. After my tension was released, I began smiling from ear to ear at the delightful revelation of this unexpected response. I complimented the reply by playing a single man game of charades, positioning my arms in the air as if I were holding an imaginary basketball at the final seconds of the playoffs, flicked my wrist like Michael Jordan hitting a jump shot at the buzzer and saying, "Swish!" After my celebratory reaction, I told God, "I don't feel comfortable being enlightened with this awareness; it's too big of a responsibility for me to disseminate this information, if that's your agenda. What am I supposed to do with this?"

"It's your choice," was the answer.

Surprised, I said, "Really? So why me . . . am I special?"

"All of My creations are one of a kind," was God's final reply.

Immediately after the divine conversation, I felt like the responses to the entire dialogue were already naturally embedded into my intuition, because the explanations seemed to be in harmony and coincide with my instinctual predisposition. I just needed the deeply rooted enlightenment to surface to a higher altitude to become aware of it.

Instantly, I thought of Cat. I scrambled to assemble my phone, then Googled the contact information to the hospital and placed my call. Promptly, I asked the operator to transfer me over to the intensive care unit. The receptionist answered the phone, and I nervously asked, "How is Catharine doing?"

"Who is her doctor?" she asked.

"I'm sorry—it's Dr. Garcia," I told her.

She said, "May I ask whom I'm speaking with?"

"Michael Coachella."

"Let me page her doctor for you, Mr. Coachella."

I tried to dry swallow fluids from my mouth that weren't there. "Okay," I said with a raspy voice. I turned on the speaker to my phone and dropped it to my side, because my muscles were exhausted from the anxiety of waiting for an update on Cat's status.

The doctor finally made himself known. "Mr. Coachella?"

Without lifting the phone, I said, "Yes, it's me."

He said, "Well, Catharine's condition has upgraded tremendously, and right now she is responsive and doing very well."

Exhilarated, I began rejoicing by running and jumping up and down throughout the house, shouting, "Yes! Yes! Yes!"

After my elation, I took the phone off speaker and said, "If I was the President of the United States, I would pardon you for a lifetime of sins and give you a Public Health Distinguished Service Medal."

He chuckled and said, "You certainly have my nomination if you ever decide to run for office, but I believe it was more of what you may have said to her that encouraged her to fight. Because not long after you left, her health miraculously improved, even before we administered her new blood. We just can't understand how she recovered as she did with such low blood pressure. She's doing much better than our staff expected. This had to be some sort of a miracle, if you believe in that type of stuff."

My gleeful smile responded to his avowal. "Doctor, after what I've just gone through, I'll bear witness to all things being possible and nothing being impossible if a person believes strongly enough."

The doctor replied, "I can tell we have a kindred spirit, and from the looks of it, Catharine does too."

"You took the words right out of my mouth. So when can I come see my soulmate?" I asked.

"She's going to be here for a couple more days under our observation so that we can effectively monitor her continuing progress," he told me. "But right now, she's asleep, still recuperating from her arduous struggle. I would say for now, let's allow her to rest like Sleeping Beauty until morning. I'll stand in as your Prince Charming proxy for the time being, since I'll be here on duty the entire night. How does that sound?"

Another smile radiated on my face, as if the light came from heaven. "They say the doctor knows best, and you have proven to be the epitome of that statement. May God continue to guide your hands to do his work. Thank you, Dr. Garcia."

CHAPTER 21
CODA MONOLOGUE

Sheltered beneath the bed sheets with my arms folded behind my head and resting on my pillow, I stared at the ceiling in the quietude of my bedroom with the tiredness of a withered old soul. Exhausted, but aware enough to cogitate profoundly about my epic journey. This was a colossal, formidable struggle that ruthlessly challenged every fiber of my resilience down to the most miniscule amount of strength that I had available.

I laughed at the irony of my expectation, because I could've never imagined in a gazillion years that I would ever be an advocate on behalf of the Most High. I'd experienced a rarefied personal edification that coincidentally fulfilled my spiritual conquest, which provided a vital prerequisite to metaphorically guide me into the center of my Tootsie Pop. That unification was the connectedness that I needed to empower me with the rudimentary understanding of a mysterious God. My consciousness had me feeling like I'd reached the pinnacle of my transcendence. But I knew that was a lie, because my top had no ceiling. There's an infinite amount of space in this universe for growth and development, and I'm an insatiable human with two hundred thousand years of instinctual curiosity; therefore, I possess a ravenous appetite to acquisition answers for every enigmatical inquiry that's hidden in plain sight.

My eyes began to tighten more with sleepiness while my placid well-being authorized my conjecturing assessment. Before I feel asleep, I conceptualized an idyllic, utopian fortune of emotional prosperity for myself and my family's happiness. It was an exquisite forethought that was worth its weight in gold. With the honor and discipline of a devoted samurai warrior, I vowed to unite my family back together and forever remain loyal while loving them with an undeniable passion that could only be reproduced in Hollywood cinematic fashion.

If I never release this memoir, the world would never know of me and my personal testament of a glorious redemption. But for now, I'm humbled and pleased to say that today was a good day.

CHAPTER 22

HEDONISTIC DESTINY

One year later, we sanctioned a geographical rebirth when we relocated and moved our family into our spacious dream home in upper-middle-class suburbia. Cat and I, celebrated the sanctity of our love for each other with a *Fairytopian*-theme wedding at an attractive outdoor botanical garden, done in a luxurious southern romantic style.

On the morning of our wedding, when all the guests were present and comfortably situated at the venue, the wedding coordinator had arranged a quartette of coupled dancers to captivate the audience. Attractive women were outfitted in the eighteenth-century European fashioned puffy dresses, with oversized ballroom hand-fans, and sophisticated men were dressed like the Phantom of the Opera, adorning black capes draped over their shoulders. Together, the dancers performed a synchronized masquerade waltz ensemble to an instrumental symphony, Aram Khachaturian's "Masquerade Suite," played by a small orchestra to inaugurate the ceremony. It was an astonishing demonstration, amazingly resembling a dramatizing production of the Renaissance.

After the gorgeous presentation, a trumpet was blown to announce Cat's appearance. She arrived at the venue in a stylish four-wheeled carriage decorated with white roses pulled by two stout, bleached-white stallions. Stepping out of the coach, she wore an awe-inspiring Christian Dior wedding dress and a pair of glass slippers only to be feverishly welcomed by a crowd-pleasing applause. Thankful, she elegantly offered a gracious bow like an esteemed duchess. Her father, whom she had always adored, gently offered his hand and chaperoned his princess down the decorative botanical walkway, into a sea of encouraging guest. Our three lovely daughters were the honored flower girls, escorted by three equally charming young gentlemen. The song "Spend My Life with You" by Eric Benét, featuring the songstress Tamia, fittingly filled the atmosphere with a mellifluent composition.

Pure white and aqua blue were the coordinated colors, which we agreeably chose to be the symbolic nature of our wedding to anew our love for each other. White was the color Cat selected for its ideal representation of clarity and its association with new beginnings. I had chosen the color aqua for its ideal representation of protection, and its association with the calming elements it would bring to our space. We also chose the number five for the total of bridesmaids and an equal quantity of accompanying groomsmen to signify the exciting adventure the quintupling digit represents for our future journey. Correspondingly, the new family pet pooch, Rocka, was an essential part of our wedding ensemble also. Dressed to impress in the official colors, she "doggedly" escorted the diamond ring on her collar as a necklet charm down the aisle through the admiring gazes.

Once the ceremonial vows were exchanged to solidify our unification, the officiating reverend performed a mock coronation sacrament and provided us a dazzling set of king and queen crowns as headdresses. After the pageantry, three hundred indigenous butterflies were released into the sky to conclude the nuptial ceremony. Instead of the traditional open-top vintage Rolls Royce classic with whitewall tires, we were provided an azure-colored

Lamborghini Murciélago for me to drive the bride to the reception hall to greet our awaiting guests.

On our arrival to the manor, a spokesman gave us an imperial introduction before entering the chamber by announcing, "Hear ye! Hear ye! Without further ado, your King and Queen of the hour have just arrived, and it's my pleasure to introduce to you . . . the new Mr. and Mrs. Coachella!"

Everyone in attendance stood and honored us enthusiastically, with clapping hand-praises as we graced the dance floor to showcase our bride and groom victory dance to the upbeat Katy Perry song "Firework" that the DJ played. Some of our guests joined us on the floor in a circlet and enriched our surroundings with money to represent a gracious symbol of prosperity.

After our dance, we made our way to the royal thrones that awaited us at the head of the ballroom to accentuate our temporal eminence. Sculpted ice angels were carved with careful details and placed throughout the room to enchant the occasion with an eye-pleasing angelic allure. Our royal court also had a jester in attendance, dressed in a Medieval costume to entertain us with juggling, magic and acrobatics.

One of the city's most celebrated comedians was employed to host and emcee the event, bringing a fulfilling dosage of laughter to the attendees. After a round of lighthearted jokes, an ambrosia feast was served by a host of professional caterers with the utmost delicacy that excited an epicurean conversation. After the decadent dinner, we stood before a breathtaking, five-tier cake and began cutting slices to accommodate our three hundred guests. While I assisted in divvying up the mouthwatering *sugarlicious* delight, someone from the staff whispered to me that Security was having an issue with a gentleman not on the register who was very determined to enter the banquet.

"Tell them if he's not on the register, to turn him away easily," I said.

"They has tried several times, but this person is very persistent." she replied.

"Do you know the person's name?" I asked.

"No," she said, "he wouldn't give me his name."

"Okay, I'll be out there in a second," I said, and told my bride I'd be right back.

I went into the lobby and came face-to-face with my father. In shock, I said, "What are you doing here, Jack?"

He said, "Son, I know I'm not welcome, but can you give me a moment?"

"Hell, no," I told him. "You swindled your opportunity."

"Well, can you tell me if you've been receiving my correspondence?" he asked.

I said, "Sure I got 'em . . . right before I shredded them. It means nothing to me, just like you . . . as a matter of fact, who in the hell told you about my wedding anyway? They're getting the fuck out of here right now, just like you."

He was afflicted with a moment of hesitancy and then he said, "That's really not important."

I was even more upset that he wouldn't reveal the Judas who had whispered to him of my wedding. I pointed at him with an uncompromising finger and said, "Who fuckin' told you?"

"Okay, it was your mother . . . but she didn't mean any harm. For a while, she wouldn't answer my calls or tell me anything about you until recently, when she told me you were getting married."

Extremely disappointed in her, I said, "Damn, Mama, why'd you do that?"

He said, "She knows that you still hurt from how I treated you, and I can see that you're carrying the scars of my inadequacies of being a father, and I'm hurting now because you've been hurting for so long. I'm sorry, Son, and I was a sorry father to you."

"You got that right." I said.

"At the time, I believed my sole responsibility was providing a roof over your head, and that buying you bikes and stuff was enough," he told me.

I abruptly said, "You simple motherfucker . . . affection is the best gift that a parent can give a child. It's the smallest thing that could fill the largest package. But instead, you provided me the toughness I needed in this cold world, so thank you, but don't beat your chest like you're King Kong because that trait was built out of my fear of a domineering parental bully by default."

"I raised you the way my father raised me, which I understand now was a mistake. When you were growing up, I wasn't as sharp as you are now to understand and know any better back then, but now I get it."

"I don't give a thousand shits if you never get it!" I said. Then I shook my head. "When I was growing up, it was weird, you know. Physically, we were close—we had to share the same space—but the emotional element somehow was never there. I was an insecure kid who needed his father's approval, and you never gave me that. So I had to find endorsements for my manhood without you. I stopped waiting for you to become that father figure I needed a long time ago."

I looked at him with disdain, poked my chest out like a Minotaur, and held my arms out to demonstrate my show of strength. "Look at me now . . . it's way too late, man."

"Yeah, you look good," he said. "You grew up to be a strong man, and I wished that I had done more to help groom you during your development."

I put my arms down, placed my hands on my hips, and started pacing in circles because I was getting even more upset.

He opened his chops and said, "I'm sure you have a beautiful family, and I have never met them. I was hoping—"

I stopped patrolling, cut him off, and said, "And you never will! Look, I told you that you're not wanted here, so pull a Houdini and pop smoke. Now beat it, before I break your ribs with a donkey punch and have Security throw your ass out!"

To my surprise, he held up his arms, exposing his ribcage and said, "Come on, hit me—I deserve it!"

I clutched my fist strongly and started breathing heavily like a raging bull with the idea of fracturing his skeletal midsection and make him whimper like a little child. But then I looked into his eyes and saw myself as the helpless, frightened boy that I used to be and felt sorry for the man I'd fantasized about hurting most of my life.

I guess he sensed my change of heart, and he lowered his arms with a teary eye and said, "Son, I know it's late, but if I could . . . I would like to purchase your forgiveness with the admission of guilt along with my sentence of shame for letting you down. I promise if you can sell me your forgiveness, I'll make it my destiny to build a bond with you out of the strongest material that has ever been created by man. I'm willing to do anything to have you back, and I don't care how crazy or ridiculous it is. I'd swim across the Atlantic Ocean, travel barefoot to Great Britain to pull Excalibur out of its stone, and slay the dragon if I thought it would give me the slightest chance of nurturing the father-and-son relationship we've never had. I desperately need you and your family in my life. I'll never let you down again, so please give me your blessings by extending me this opportunity."

I felt my defensive prowess start to weaken, and I said, "Man, you should have been a salesman . . . why did you have to mention *Excalibur*—you know that's my favorite movie?"

"I've watched that movie at least a hundred times since you went away . . . and I'm a dreamer as well. It's *our* favorite movie, Son."

I extended my arms out like I was Moses parting the Red Sea that separated us and said, "Come here!"

We embraced, and I fantasized I was a child all over again just for that instant. It was a feeling that I've longed for my entire life.

I pulled away, wiped a tear from my cheek, and said, "Come on, man, you can't be doing this. Got a king sensitive on his wedding day—don't you know that's sacrilegious? I might lose my kingship over this."

He said, "Even without that crown, you'll be a better ruler than King Arthur."

I smiled and placed my arm around my father, turned to the security guys, and said, "All right, a king and his father is about to make a royal entrance into the world of Camelot... can you please open the door, gentlemen, so that we may proceed."

When we made our way inside the banquet hall, I asked my father to locate an available seat anywhere inside and told him that I would introduce him to my family after the event. I orbited around the dance floor, where people were dancing and enjoying the sound of music, to my throne, where Cat was anticipating my return. She asked me, "Who's the older guy that came in with you?"

"He's an honored guest," I said. "You'll find out soon."

Before the wedding, I'd purchased several packets of Ferrero Rocher chocolates to account for every day we were apart, and had them delivered to the kitchen inside the banquet hall earlier that morning. With Cat oblivious to what I'd arranged, and while everyone was reveling in conversation all across the room, I signaled to the staff for the chocolates to be rolled in on a pushcart right in front of us. On its arrival, Cat took a glance at all the chocolate, elevated to her feet, and then looked at me and said, "I can't believe you remembered!"

Rising to my feet. "I bet you can't eat just one."

She said, "I'm going to try, but it's going to be all your fault if I mess up this beautiful wedding dress."

"Good luck," I said.

"You better hope I don't lose this bet," she told me, "I'm going to haunt you as a honeymoon gift if I die on my wedding day from a chocolate overdose."

I firmly grabbed both of her hands and gently said, "Sweetheart, you wouldn't imagine what I did to get you back into my life when you were dying, so please don't make any references of leaving me again."

"What did you do?" she asked.

I looked away for a moment to contemplate giving her a quick synopsis about the difficult topic, but I didn't believe that she would understand or relate with the extreme fervor I felt was necessary to exude. I then took a more assertive position and looked softly into her eyes and said, "It's complicated. I'm sorry that I can't find the words right now to tell you, and I don't think I ever could. Just know that I love you, and I did something incredible."

"Well," she said, "I trust that you did something that's honorable, because God has surely been blessing us."

"You sure right." I said.

"Okay, I love you too." She gave me a hug and then turned and went in the direction of the pushcart.

While Cat was at the wagon eating chocolates, Ronnie walked up and handed me a gift bag. "This belongs to you."

I peeked inside and asked, "What's this?"

He motioned over to the Russian who was in attendance. Nikolay came over and said, "You must be doing something right, because this is one spectacular wedding—and that, my friend, is your thirty-one thousand dollars minus my fifty percent commission, which of course I've already exercised the liberty of making the appropriate deduction."

I looked down and noticed that he was wearing a pair of handcrafted, pointy-arch designer boots with silver-plated toe tips—which could've only belonged to one person. I turned to Ronnie and said, "How did you know?"

"There is more to something than meets the eye." he said. Then he closed his eyes, revealing his ink. "These tattoos are a symbolic gesture of my cognitive foresight; I often see things people don't want to be seen. I hope you didn't think I would allow Cowboy to get away with ripping off my organization and my brother. I'm the patriarch of the Archangels . . . our duty is to maintain equilibrium in the four corners of the universe; balancing the good and the evil within my sovereignty is my responsibility. Justice can get extremely poetic, and that's why it was critical for me to get Nikolay involved. He also specializes in sophisticated matters like this."

"Well, getting some of my money back is great," I said, "but I didn't want him murdered!"

He said, "Your conscious is clear—I said poetic, not exterminated! I asked Nikolay to be creative, so he assured me that Cowboy will be taking an atypical leave of absence in Siberia indefinitely."

I turned to Nikolay and asked, "How did you manage to do that? Another thing . . . other than it being a desolate place, what makes his deportation unusual?"

He replied, "Like I told you before, I'm a man with international resources, even in societies with inhospitable weather." He adjusted his custom-made suit like he was Vito Corleone from *The Godfather* before he continued. "But he, this Cowboy, he's a very mysterious fella—even I couldn't trace his background of where the fuck he came from or the origins of his birth with my Interpol connections that can identify anyone on the planet with state-of-the-art technology."

My lips separated like the San Andreas Fault line. "Whoa!" I was taken back, because I'd believed that at least everything Cowboy told me about his extensive ancestral lineage was factual.

Nikolay then reached in his breast pocket and pulled out a Cuban cigar that was personalized with Cowboy's initials stamped on it. He used it like a virtuoso holding a baton to accent his next point when he said, "I think you should research the meaning of his assumed Egyptian name when you get the opportunity, because it's probably not far from the truth of what it suggests."

I wasn't sure what Nikolay was implying at the time, but I said, "All right." Then he said, "He's one tough son of a bitch, that guy. The crazy bastard enjoyed everything my guys put him through; I've never seen anything like it in my life. He literally has to be the devil, so what better place on earth than Siberia to keep little Satan on ice?"

It was a challenging endeavor for me to visualize what type of abominable condition Cowboy was in. Cat then walked up and interrupted my dreamy, torturous production of Cowboy's situation with a chocolate avalanche around the rim of her mouth and dripping off her fingers, saying, "Look what you did."

We just started laughing, and I looked over at the cart and saw a plethora of empty wrappers. "Wow," I said, surprised, "how did you manage to eat that many so quick?" With her hands extended out so as not to stain her dress, she said, "You challenged me, and I lost. My stomach hurts, baby—you have to do something."

"I'm sorry, sweetheart," I said, "but there's no cure or relief for chocolate-itis."

"Stop teasing and help me." she said.

I motioned for one of the waitrons to come over and assist in cleaning Cat's areas of concern with linen napkins. When the attendant left, Cat noticed the bag I was holding and said, "If you have more chocolates in that bag to challenge me with, I'm going to have vomit-itis all over my wedding dress. I think we've made it clear that I can't eat just one."

I opened up the bag and leaned over to show Cat what was inside and then I said, "What you think about having cash-itis?"

Cat said, "Michael, where did all this money come from?"

I looked over and nodded at the Russian, then looked back at Cat and said, "Beloved, I'm sorry—this is a friend of ours named Nikolay."

Nikolay reached for Cat's hand like a gentleman and said, "Mrs. Coachella, I am extremely pleased to meet such a beautiful woman, and together you two look exceptionally presidential."

"That is a benevolent compliment; I'm speechless," Cat replied.

I intervened, telling him, "What she means is, thank you. We're grateful for your generous gift." I then looked at Cat and said, "This is a serendipitous moment . . . I don't know about you babe, but I feel like we've won the Grand Prix."

Cat reached into the bag with both hands and pulled out bundles of wrapped legal tender and said, "What are we going to do with all of this?"

"We're going to take a scenic cruise across the ocean for our honeymoon in Barcelona," I told her.

Cat closed her eyes, grabbed her head, and said, "Oh, ole."

"What's wrong?" I asked.

"I'm having that déjà vu feeling again; I think I'm hallucinating."

I smiled and said, "This is no illusion, baby; it's the fantasy we've always dreamt of that has finally came true, but this story will never end."

Cat opened up her eyes. "You gave me back my center, Michael, even more than I could've ever imagined . . . I love you deeply, baby."

While we kissed, Nikolay called over a cocktail waitress to pour us all a drink and said, "Let's have a toast and salute to a matrimony that will survive the end of time."

We held our glasses in the air and shouted, "Yeah!"

www.ingramcontent.com/pod-product-compliance
Lightning Source LLC
LaVergne TN
LVHW051044080426
835508LV00019B/1698